The JOHN WAYNE Story

John Wayne in *Cahill*
(Warner Brothers, 1973)

The
JOHN
WAYNE
Story

By

GEORGE CARPOZI Jr.

ROBERT HALE · LONDON

© 1972 by George Carpozi, Jr.
First published in Great Britain 1974

ISBN 0 7091 4449 0

Robert Hale & Company
63 Old Brompton Road,
London, S.W.7

B|WAY.

HERTFORDSHIRE
COUNTY LIBRARY
HEMH
791.430280924
6213669

Printed in Great Britain by
Lowe & Brydone (Printers) Ltd,
Thetford, Norfolk

Contents

6

Fore*warning*

An old colleague on the Hearst Newspapers, cartoonist Jimmy Hatlo, used to do a feature called, "They'll Do It Every Time."

If I may take a "loanout" on that phrase, I'd like to predict regarding this book—my fifteenth—that some reviewers will be as critical as they were about each of my other fourteen tomes, saying that I *"failed to capture the real . . ."* John Wayne, that this biography is only a "superficial study," and perhaps even an "injustice" to the most imposing movie actor of our time.

Frankly, I don't give a damn what the reviewers say. Nor, for that matter, what the readers think. My only concern is what John "Duke" Wayne himself thinks. He's the guy I'm most scared of because I ain't in any hurry, no-how, to have him git mad at me agin . . .

Illustrations

John Wayne in *Cahill* (Warner Brothers, 1973) *Frontispiece*

Between pages 87 and 96
John Wayne and Esperanza Baur
With his son Michael
Kiss for Esperanza
At divorce hearing
Studies in solemnity
Chata's doodles
Toni Wayne's wedding
Duke and Pilar Palette
With Aissa
The Wayne home on fire
Duke and Pilar in New York
Melinda Wayne's wedding
Marisa Carmela Wayne's camera debut
With John Ethan Wayne, aged three
With Marisa, aged two
A trio of Waynes
With grandson Michael Ian
John Ethan, now nine

Between pages 140 and 149
Portraits 1937, 1940 and 1942
In *Back to Bataan* (1945)
A rugged moment in *The Alamo* (1960)
As General Sherman in *How the West Was Won* (1964)
Filming in *The Sons of Katie Elder* (1965)

CHAPTER I

"Meet John Wayne," She Said, and How I Did . . . Terrified!

It was during the 1966 *Photoplay* Magazine Awards at the Hotel Manhattan. "I want you to meet John Wayne," said Mary Fiore, the editor of *Photoplay*.

At five-foot-eight, I was eye-level with his tie clip. I looked up and squinted for a glimpse of his face, which was towering above me like the observation roof of the Empire State Building.

"Glad to meet you, George," Wayne drawled, gripping my hand. That stopped the circulation in both my hands. He was clutching a Scotch on the rocks in his left hand, and even as he held onto my hand he sipped from the glass, wiped his lips with his tongue, and asked me what else I did besides serve as contributing editor to *Photoplay.*

"I'm a reporter for the *New York Post,*" I said. I had just stepped off the treadmill that was Hearst's fast-declining *New York Journal-American.*

"For the what!" Wayne growled, grimacing like Sergeant Stryker when he was shouting orders to his platoon to take the beach in *Sands of Iwo Jima.* It was not a question. It was a demand for an explanation.

No reply was necessary. Trying to tell Wayne why I worked for the *Post,* not only the nation's largest-circulation evening newspaper but the oldest continuously published daily in the country (founded by Alexander Hamilton in 1801), would have been wasted on deaf ears.

Figuratively speaking, Wayne had climbed onto a soapbox in the middle of the crowd of celebrities in the Manhattan's Playbill Bar.

"That's a goddamn left-wing pinko rag," he thundered. "Anyone gets himself tied up with a crummy paper like that must be a stinkin' punk. I got no use for anybody who works for a no-good sheet like that. I wouldn't trust you for nothin', workin' for that Commie rag. You must be desperate to do anything like that . . ."

His hand went to my throat as he ranted and raved about my newspaper. He tightened his fingers around my collar and shook me back and forth.

"I'm going to walk away from you now," he said, taking another slug of Scotch, "and I don't ever want to see ya again, ya crum . . ."

Then, after one final back-and-forth thrust, he relinquished his hold on my throat, turned on his heels, strutted away—on the bias—and headed back to the bar.

Mary Fiore, who'd witnessed the scene, broke into a laugh.

"He's not mad at you," Mary told me. "He just doesn't like your newspaper."

"Oh," I said, "I'm so relieved. Now tell that to my throat and we'll see if the pain goes away . . ."

For the next couple of hours, I sat at *Photoplay*'s table chatting with other Hollywood celebrities.

Along about midnight, Wayne—he had passed my table several times during the evening, always with a drink in hand and always glaring at me, his lips mumbling taunting phrases—finally returned. He put his hand on my shoulder, took a fistful of my jacket into his catcher's-mitt grip, and yanked me out of my chair.

"You're on the wrong set," I trembled. "We're not shooting the saloon fight scene until tomorrow . . ."

"Awww, come on," Wayne drawled. "I'm not really sore at *you*."

He *whupped* his arm around me, cuddled me against his barrel chest, and held me there until I began to experience the onset of asphyxia. Then he relaxed his hold and put his glass to my lips.

"Come on, pal," he smiled, "have a drink with me."

He forced me to swallow a mouthful of Scotch and then said:

"You know somethin'? I got nothin' against you . . . it's just that I don't like the goddamn paper you work for."

Then he shook my hand.

"We're friends, right?" he asked.

"Yup," I said, sounding like a vest pocket Gary Cooper.

"Awright, pal," Wayne came back, his arm around me again. "You're going with me to the bar because I'm buyin' ya a drink . . ."

People who witnessed the scenes between Wayne and me that night, and others who heard about them, have asked why I would want to write his biography and add to the John Wayne legend.

"Why not," I've been asked, "target on some other movie star—someone who, maybe, appreciates and respects you (and your newspaper) more?"

My answer is simple. Since I couldn't punch him in the nose—because it was so far out of my reach—I've chosen this way to get back.

This is being written so all the world can see the real John Wayne. In the language of the newspaperman, this is the *who, what, when, where, how,* and *why* of the Iowa-born boy who became the two-fisted hero of America's box offices, who has been admired and revered by two generations of movie-goers, and who today stands as one of Hollywood's very few all-time superstars.

I hope the book shakes him up as much as he shook me that night. Those of you who've read my biographies of Brigitte Bardot, Marilyn Monroe, Clark Gable, Vince Edwards, Jacqueline Kennedy, Gary Cooper, and Johnny Cash know my style. I shoot from the hip and hit 'em between the eyes. For I dig for the truth and handle it as J. Swartz once wrote:

"Truth without charity is often intolerant and even persecuting, as charity without truth is weak in concession and untrustworthy in judgment. —But charity, loyal to truth and rejoicing in it, has the wisdom of the serpent with the harmlessness of the dove."

This is John Wayne's story. Much of it has tumbled from his own lips. Much of it has been related by those who've been nearest and dearest to him—and who've known him best.

This is John Wayne's story but, more significantly, it is the story of John Wayne . . .

CHAPTER II

Days on the Farm

Thirty miles out of Des Moines there's a small Iowa town called Winterset. To most folks, the name may be as familiar as Cadiz, Ohio. Yet both towns are rightly entitled to fame, for they produced two of the most representative he-men this country has ever known. Cadiz's gift to the world was Clark Gable. Winterset's was Marion Michael Morrison.

Who's that, you ask?

Well, as John Wayne put it many years later, that was a "very severe name to inflict on a boy." But that happened to be the monicker Wayne's parents used on his birth certificate, which was issued on May 26, 1907. He didn't have a leathery skin then, but his eyes were blue and they had the same look of a sad and friendly hound that they have today.

16

Wayne has never been sure whether this description of his eyes is a compliment. But he doesn't mind it because he's always been fond of dogs.

"If you want to know the truth," Wayne has admitted, "I don't think I'm exactly ugly, yet I don't imagine I'll ever win any beauty prizes. My father was better looking as a baby and as a man than I am . . ."

Clyde Morrison, who was of Scottish descent and about as husky as Wayne is today but a shade under six feet tall, had settled in Winterset around the turn of the century, as best as Wayne can recall, and opened what was the town's leading drugstore. There were no others, in fact.

Wayne's father was a registered pharmacist but he did more than dispense drugs. Known to the townspeople as "Doc," he gave advice on any and all problems brought to him by his customers.

"He handed out his homespun philosophy without charge, along with the prescriptions he compounded for his customers," Wayne explained. "That is, he often didn't get paid for the drugs either because he hated to press his customers to pay their bills."

Wayne describes his father as the "kindest, most patient man [he] ever met," saying that the elder Morrison never had an unkind thought in his mind and rarely spoke harshly to his son or anyone else. Nor did he ever lecture young Marion. But he did teach him three stringent rules for living which have the ring of orders tumbling from the lips of Davy Crockett in the nineteenth century:

1. Always keep your word.
2. A gentleman never insults anybody intentionally.
3. Don't go around looking for trouble. But if you ever get in a fight, make sure you win it.

I must assume then that when John Wayne gave me the

working over that night at the *Photoplay* Awards, he either:
1. Was not a gentleman.
2. Insulted me *un*intentionally.

I have no doubt that he could have executed the third rule of life preached by his father.

Marion Michael's mother, Mary Margaret Brown, was the extreme opposite of his father. Descended from sturdy Irish stock, she was, as Wayne described her, "a tiny, vivacious, red-headed bundle of energy" who, he always thought, resembled the late Billie Burke.

"I think I inherited my size [six feet, four inches] from my mother's side," Wayne said. "Her father was all of six-feet-three . . . but I'll never understand why Mom didn't grow any taller."

Memories of his days in Winterset are hazy, for the boy who was Marion Michael Morrison spent only the first six years of his life there. Yet he can recall a few highlights of that period with fondness.

"I remember riding horses and playing football . . . damn, did I like football," Wayne said wistfully. "I just wanted to play it all the time."

Marion Michael had one experience in Winterset that he'll never forget. It happened shortly after his brother, Robert, was born in 1910.

"I went in to see little Bobby, rubbed my shoes on the rug, and accidentally touched the metal foot of the bed," Wayne recalled. "Sparks shot off. I thought I had found one of the wonders of the universe. I didn't know that Benjamin Franklin had beaten me to the discovery by about 150 years."

The Summers in Winterset were pleasant and the clear, clean air imposed no hardships on anyone's lungs. Not even Clyde Morrison's. But when Winter came it was another story. Doc could hardly breathe the cold, damp air, which assaulted his lungs with the chill, penetrating sting of a mentholated cigarette.

The family doctor, whom Morrison seldom consulted, finally reached him with these words of advice:

"Clyde, your lungs are in bad shape. You're not going to get rid of that congestion. I don't want to see you come down with consumption. I've got just one suggestion for you, and I think you'd better take it—go West, young man."

"I remember how much my Dad suffered," Wayne said. "He was coughing and hacking all the time. And to make it worse, he was always bushed. He'd drag himself into his drugstore early in the morning and drag himself out late at night and he'd hardly have the strength left to crawl into bed."

One day, when Doc could barely speak during a siege of racking coughs, he announced to his wife:

"Molly, I'm going out to California and look around for a new home for us. I can't take it here anymore."

Morrison sold his drugstore for what Wayne described as "peanuts" and went searching for a new homestead in Southern California. Six months later he returned home and explained in more detail what he had written piecemeal to his family while he was scouting the "new frontier."

"I got us an eighty-acre farm on a homesteading basis and I built a farmhouse," Morrison told his wife and sons. Marion and Bob jumped for joy.

"We've gonna live on a farm, we're gonna live on a farm!" Marion shouted. "We can ride horses and play cowboys and Indians! Yahoo!"

When the family arrived on the "farm" in Palmdale, situated on the fringes of the unfriendly Mojave Desert, they found that the "farmhouse" their father had built was hardly more than a glorified shack. The land itself was nothing but cactus and sagebrush—with rattlers outnumbering the hundreds of "friendly" jackrabbits.

But to the Morrisons, snakes and hares were enemies of equal magnitude. As Wayne says, they were "squatters who had lain claim to our property and threatened to stop us from raising crops. So we went out there and shot them like fish in a barrel."

Bob was too small to help but Marion wasn't. He was at his dad's side from daybreak to dusk clearing the cactus and sagebrush— and shooting the rattlesnakes and rabbits—to prepare the land for planting. Fortunately, since rain is almost unheard of in Palmdale and other regions of the Mojave Desert, the Morrisons did not have to drill very deep to reach the water table, and with a good-sized pump they obtained an adequate supply of water for irrigation.

The chief crop of other farms in the area around Palmdale and nearby Lancaster was alfalfa. Those who didn't till the soil raised cattle. But none of that for Morrison. He was from Iowa and he wanted to grow corn.

"Dad put forty acres in corn," Wayne recalls. "It was the only thing he could do because he couldn't afford those damn expensive farm machines needed for other types of crops."

How was the corn harvested, Wayne was asked?

"Christ, I bet I husked more ears by hand than any kid who ever lived," he said. "I think I still have the callouses on my hands from those days. But Dad did his share of the work, too."

Those were difficult times for the Morrisons.

"It was a hard life and we were living close to the margin of starvation," Wayne reminisced. "Mostly we ate potatoes or beans in one form or another. If we had anything else, it amounted to a rare treat."

Wayne vividly recalls one Halloween when his mother gave the family a big treat—frankfurters and beans.

"All of us except Dad sat down. Dad hadn't come home yet. In the middle of the table was the big bowl of weiners. As we waited for Dad, there was a scratching noise at the window. I got up and opened the door. Standing beside the house was a white shadow.

" 'A ghost!' I told myself. I ran back to the table, grabbed the bowl of franks, and heaved it at the Halloween intruder . . ."

Not only did he give his playful trick-or-treating father a lump on the head but, Wayne said, he "ruined a perfectly fine sheet that Dad had draped over himself to scare us kids."

That night Mrs. Morrison "scared" up a substitute supper. Potatoes, as usual.

Life on the farm provided Marion Michael with his first really memorable youthful thrill in riding a horse. It was not just galloping around the farm but much more.

"Our horse was named Jenny," Wayne said, "and if I could be as kind as I possibly could I would say, at best, she was an exhausted brown mare. But I loved her more than anything in the world."

Man O' War would have been exhausted by the amount of exercise Jenny was given by Marion Michael.

The nearest grade school for Marion was in Lancaster, eight miles from home. Walking was out, and it was up to

Jenny to be his "school bus." He rode the mare to classes and back. Twice a week he'd also stop at the general store in Lancaster for a sack of groceries and staples, which he roped to his back with his schoolbooks.

Saddling up on Jenny required no lessons. Marion Michael had learned to ride a mount back in Iowa. "Riding a horse always came as natural to me as breathing," Wayne says with pride. But he didn't begin playing cowboy on horseback until he rode Jenny to school. He was barely seven years old.

On the way back from class, Marion Michael's trail took him over unpaved roads that were nothing but caked mud and gray-red rocks. But the terrain was made to order for the youngster's daily excursion into fantasy.

"As I trotted home late in the afternoon, sometimes with the supplies and books lashed to my shoulder, I'd come to that there place in the road where it made a sharp turn around the Goddamnest cliff you ever saw. I'd pretend there was a gang of outlaws lying around the bend, waiting to ambush me.

"I somehow managed to scare myself to death, almost, and pretend I always picked up a carcass full of lead. Then I'd dig my heels into Jenny and she'd gallop down the road. The outlaws were never there, of course. Nobody was there. All I ever ran across were a few scrubby palms, some mesquite, packs of jackrabbits, and a few lazy rattlesnakes."

When Marion Michael Morrison finally did run into outlaws behind a cliff, it was twenty years later.

"And then," Wayne laughed while telling this, "I was the hero in the picture—so I always managed to kill those buzzards before they killed me."

Despite the many hardships of farm life and the frequent

encounters with near-starvation experienced by the Morrisons, Marion Michael never knew the meaning of heartbreak and suffering until he was eight. Then he sustained an emotional tragedy that scarred him for life.

Jenny, who was never endowed with an overabundance of vitality, began to lose what little she had. Her frail frame grew frailer—until, as Wayne puts it, "she was nothing but bones and hide."

"The more oats I gave her, the thinner and weaker she grew. The folks in Lancaster who saw Jenny tied up outside the school thought I wasn't feeding her enough, or mistreating her. They complained to the local humane society, or something that passed for it, and they sent somebody over to the school to complain to my teacher. But she stood up for me like my own mother. She told the man that nobody takes care of his horse the way I do."

But Jenny's condition continued to deteriorate. Finally, Marion's father brought her to the veterinarian in Lancaster who examined the old mare and found no way to save her.

"She's dying and it's a pity to let her suffer," the vet told the elder Morrison.

"Does that mean she's gotta be shot?" Marion asked, his voice choking.

That's what it meant—and Jenny was destroyed.

"I've never gotten over that experience," Wayne said. "Jenny was a part of me and when they took her away, hell, it was just like cutting my arm or leg off."

In years to come, when Marion Michael grew up to be John Wayne, movie star and hero of Western sagas, he had an inordinate compassion for horses. In more film productions than he can remember, he said, he was the horses' leading champion.

"If I saw a guy mistreating a horse," Wayne related with a grimace, "I'd go to him and say, 'If you wanna treat that mount that way, then you're gonna have to expect me to show you how it feels.' "

Jenny's demise left Marion Michael without transportation. Since his father couldn't afford the price of another horse, young Morrison, now eight years old, had to rely on a neighbor to take him to classes on the back of an old buckboard.

"That also finished my encounters with the bad guys down at the pass," Wayne said with sadness. "It wasn't until a couple of years later that I really got to play cowboy again. But it wasn't the same because I didn't have a horse. You didn't need a horse where I was then . . ."

CHAPTER III

They Named Him "Duke"

John Wayne, or Marion Michael Morrison, would have been the one to tell his father that he wasn't cut out to be a farmer—if his mother hadn't said it first.

"Two years on the farm, crop failure after crop failure, misery and more misery," said Wayne. "Mom was getting fed up fast. She and Dad had many bitter discussions. He wanted to stay, she wanted to leave. Some of their arguments were so severe I thought they'd bust up their marriage. She told him he wasn't fit for agriculture. It took a long time, but he finally agreed. By then his savings were down next to nothing."

For the first time in his life, Clyde Morrison became an employee. He went to work as a pharmacist in Glendale, California, one of the many sprawling suburbs of Los Angeles—not nearly as thickly populated and built-up then as it is today. The drugstore where he worked was not far from the small one-family home he had rented on Louise Street —and not too distant from the Triangle Studios, one of the silent era's many motion picture producers churning out one-a-day two-reel Westerns.

Though he was making a respectable thirty dollars a week, Doc Morrison had no extra money left after payday for luxuries. Anything that remained when household expenses and rent were paid, Morrison stashed away for a goal.

Meanwhile, his parents put Marion Michael on notice. If he wanted new duds, he'd have to earn the money to pay for them himself. He was eleven years old and he decided to get a job.

"I heard that the *Los Angeles Examiner* wanted kids to take paper routes," Wayne said. "I applied and got the job. The *Examiner* is a morning paper, so I had to get up at 4:00 A.M. to deliver it. It wasn't a very bad deal because I was able to make nearly six dollars a week for working just a few hours each day before school. But I also had to work Saturdays and Sundays."

After two years of an existence which might be termed frugal but not impoverished, Doc Morrison had saved enough to start his own pharmacy again.

Morrison opened his drugstore in the Jensen Building in Glendale, which also housed the Glendale Theater. In no time at all, Doc became good friends with the theater manager, who gave Marion and his brother Bob carte blanche admission to his movie house.

"I took full advantage of the offer," Wayne said. "I'd go there four or five times a week—much more often than the average boy of my age who had to pay his way in."

Why did Marion Michael Morrison go to the movies so often?

"Movies fascinated me," he explained. "When *The Four Horsemen of the Apocalypse* played the Glendale, I saw it twice a day the whole week it played."

Douglas Fairbanks, Sr., was Marion Michael's favorite actor by far.

"I admired his dueling, his stunts, his fearlessness in the face of danger, and his impish grin when he was about to kiss his lady-love," Wayne confessed.

When it came time to play "movie-making," Marion Michael had his role all picked out. Because they were so near to the Triangle Studios, the kids in the neighborhood were movie-struck. They watched the two-reelers being filmed on the open lots near their neighborhood and cheered lustily as cowboys and Indians went tumbling off their horses before the cameras. Nobody complained because the noise didn't affect filming—there was no sound in those days.

"We'd gather and watch with open mouths and beating hearts," Wayne reminisced.

What Marion Michael and his friends observed in watching the scenes filmed at Triangle provided them with the experience to make their own "movies" on Louise Street.

We had actors, a director, and a cameraman," Wayne said. "The cameraman used a cigar box with holes punched in for a camera."

And whose role did Marion Michael invariably play?

"Yeah," he said, "I played Douglas Fairbanks."

Young Morrison mimicked Fairbanks every time he stepped before the "camera."

"Once," Wayne recalled, "I tried jumping out of a second-story window. As I went out, I grabbed some vines and swung like Tarzan. Cripes, did I ruin a beautiful grape arbor!"

Marion Michael and his pals preferred the cowboy-and-Indian make-believe to the Fairbanks adventure. So they made more Western "movies."

"My favorite Western stars of that time were William S. Hart, Dustin Farnum, Hoot Gibson, and Tom Mix," Wayne said. "I played them all but I liked Harry Carey the most because he looked real. Years later I had the pleasure of playing with Harry in pictures. In *Red River*, for instance, Carey played the man who bought my cattle when we ran them into Abilene."

In more recent years, Carey's son, Dobie, is John Wayne's very good friend and has appeared in many of our hero's movies.

While making those make-believe movies was an ordeal for him, the biggest trial of Marion Michael's early youth was shepherding his little brother around.

"Wherever I went," Wayne said, "Bob had to follow. Once I was invited to a girl's birthday party. I was about ten or eleven, I think. After the cake and ice cream, we started playing kissing games and somebody said, pointing to my brother, 'get that little squirt out of here!' I got goddamn mad at the remark and went up and punched the kid who said it right in the mouth."

Marion Michael was declared the winner—but he lost the fight by default.

"The girl's mother ordered me to leave the party," Wayne said.

But that didn't end the episode. Marion Michael went home, got an air rifle which he had bought from his paper route earnings, and climbed a garage roof that provided a perfect view of the patio behind the girl's house.

"I triggered off my bb's at every damn balloon that was strung up for the party—and busted every damn one," Wayne laughed.

Wayne has mentioned this episode to many interviewers over the years and has always been impelled to make one point clear.

"This was the first—and last—time I ever attempted to right a wrong with a rifle."

There is a saying that coming events cast their shadows before them. John Wayne will tell you that the first shadow of his legitimate acting career was cast at the graduation exercises commemorating his departure from Glendale Elementary School.

"There'd been a contest for the best essay," Wayne recalled. "The dubious prize was the honor of reciting the essay at graduation."

He wrote what might be called a composition on World War I. In the piece he discussed at great length the Kaiser's aggressive actions against France and various other aspects of Germany's provocations against the Allied powers.

"I broke into a hot sweat when my teacher told me I was the lucky winner," Wayne smiled, recalling the most significant part of the story.

"For days and days my teacher drilled me on the composition, which she wanted me to recite at graduation. One line in my essay read: 'And the worst thing the Germans had done . . .' Every time teacher drilled me, I left out the 'had.' Then came the big night. I was anxious to recite the line right. So anxious, in fact, that when I stood on the stage and came to the line, I looked straight at her and shouted: 'And the worst thing the Germans HAD done was . . .' "

That very instant, Marion Michael Morrison's mind went blank.

"I couldn't remember another word of that speech," Wayne said.

He remembers bowing stiffly and walking off the stage. For years afterward, whenever he visited Glendale and folks who were at the grade school graduation on that memorable night asked him what the worst thing the Germans had done was, John Wayne still didn't remember.

"It's a total blank in my mind," he says.

By the time Marion Michael had graduated grade school, almost no one called him by his proper name. To one and all he was "Duke."

Over the years, there have been a number of differing stories as to how John Wayne acquired this nickname. One version was that Wayne had played the role of a British peer —which he never did—and therefore was named Duke. There was even a tale that he was descended from British nobility.

"What a lot of crap those stories are," said Wayne. "Why nobody wants to go with the damn truth, I'll never understand."

The nickname really dates back to when Wayne was in the eighth grade. He had gotten a large Airedale named Duke.

"This dog," explained Wayne, "was crazy about fire-houses. Every chance he got, he sneaked away and ran over to one of the firehouses. So, whenever he was missing, I'd go to the firehouses to look for him. All the firemen knew him. They didn't know my name, but they knew the dog's. So, when I'd come around looking for my dog, they'd call me Duke, too."

During the Summer following graduation from grade school, Marion Michael Morrison worked at a number of jobs. Primarily, he was his father's number-one delivery boy. He delivered drug orders on his bicycle. He also got a spare-time job hauling ice for the local iceman. After he entered high school he also worked as an apricot picker and a truck driver.

In the fall of 1921 two significant things happened. Marion Michael's parents separated and he entered Glendale Union High School. Marion and Bob stayed with their mother, but they saw their father often.

When the call went out in the high school for football practice, Marion Michael was one of the first to report.

"I was crazy about football," Wayne said, "and I was getting so tall and strong that I knew I could handle any position on the team."

The coach looked him over and put him through a few drills. Marion Michael executed best as a running guard. That was the position the coach assigned to him.

His performance on the freshman team was so outstanding that Marion Michael won a starting role on the varsity squad in his sophomore year. By the time he played his last game as a senior, his team had won the Southern California Scholastic Football Championship and the University of Southern California had offered him an athletic scholarship.

But Marion Michael's ambition was to embark on a career in the Navy. More than anything, he wanted to be accepted by the U.S. Naval Academy.

"I wanted to spend my life in the Navy," Wayne said, "but the people who pick the candidates for Annapolis never got around to me. I finished fourth in the tests given to some thirty applicants and I had to settle for the USC scholarship."

Years later, Wayne remarked:

"It was the best thing that ever happened to me . . ."

His scholarship covered tuition but nothing else.

"So I washed dishes in the fraternity house for my meals," Wayne explained, "but I still didn't have money to pay for such things as shoes, suits, laundry, and buying pretty girls ice cream sodas at the sweet shoppe."

He decided to work for the California Bell Telephone Company, which had an opening for a "map plotter." The job paid sixty cents an hour but to this day Wayne doesn't really understand what he did to earn this pay.

"I sat in front of a map and charted where the old telephone lines ran before they were moved," he said. "But I'll be damned if I was gonna argue with them so long as they paid me that sixty cents an hour."

Meanwhile, Marion Michael's father's new drugstore had failed and Doc Morrison decided to embark upon another venture—ice cream manufacturing. But this enterprise folded, too, and Marion's dad opened another drugstore, and when this went out of business he started a paint manufacturing concern, which also went under. Despite his succession of reverses, Doc Morrison unfailingly sent his son five dollars a week.

"In return," Wayne related, "I would send Dad one of the two football tickets I was allotted because he was a hell of a fan. Of course, I never let on that he was costing me twenty dollars a week."

The two tickets that Coach Howard Jones handed out to each of the forty athletes on his squad were worth twenty-five dollars on the black market. Like most of his teammates, Marion Michael could have sold both tickets for half a hundred. But he would sell only one ticket because he wanted his father to have the other—even if it cost him twenty dollars every week during the football season. His loss, after all, was minimized by the five dollars a week his father was sending.

At the end of his freshman year at USC, Marion Michael got bad news from the phone company.

"Seems they had run out of maps to plot," Wayne said. "And the sad part of it was that I desperately needed money."

Coach Jones called his star pupil over one day before Summer recess.

"Duke," said Jones, "I hear you need a Summer job."

"I sure do," Marion Michael replied.

"Well," Jones said, "I have one for you. Last season I got Tom Mix a good box for the games. He said if there was ever anything he could do for me he would do it. I'm sending some of the squad over to the William Fox Studios. Mr. Mix will get you boys jobs."

The next morning, Marion Michael and another USC player, Don Williams, hustled over to the old Fox lot on Western Avenue and located Tom Mix, the era's top money-making star who was pulling down $17,500 a week. Hollywood's leading luminary was on a set built like the main street of a frontier town.

"Men," Mix addressed Marion and Don who stood shaking in front of him, "a star owes it to his public to keep in fine physical condition. I want you to be my trainers. I'm sure you will appreciate the benefits not only to me but to yourselves. Because when you have helped to keep me in shape, you will have remained in shape for your sport, which I understand is football."

Marion Michael and Don Williams thought Mix was a bit

of an eccentric—but the offer to work for one of filmdom's greatest stars was overpowering. They agreed.

"Greed is more like it," Wayne said. "I was hungry to make money and the offer Tom Mix made was just too damn good to pass up."

Mix's last words to the two gridmen from USC were: "Report to me personally when school is over."

A fortnight later, Marion Michael Morrison went on his own to see Tom Mix. He got as far as the front gate at the studio, but couldn't get past the guard.

Minutes later, Mix pulled up in a chauffeur-driven Locomobile which, according to Wayne, appeared to be "two blocks long." Young Marion Michael smiled at the cowboy superstar and called out, "Hello, Mr. Mix, sir."

Mix vaguely nodded. That was the last encounter Marion Michael ever had with Tom Mix. But Mix kept his promise to Coach Howard Jones—word was sent to the gateman to have Marion Michael report to the "swing gang" inside.

"My first reaction," said Wayne, "was that Tom Mix was giving me the business. But when I reported to the guy that was running things, a fellow named George Marshall, I changed my mind. He told me I was gonna get thirty-five dollars a week, which was more money that I or anybody in my family had ever made working for other people."

The job itself sounded important but all it meant was that Marion Michael would carry furniture and props around and arrange them on the set. Marshall sent the new employe to Lefty Hugg, assistant director to John Ford, who was shooting *Mother Machree*. The set was a small street in an Irish village and the star of the film was Victor McLaglen.

"Go down to the prop department and get me a flock of

geese and ducks!" Ford shouted to the newest member of the "swing gang." Marion Michael scooted aimlessly toward the edge of the set. One of the hands said to him, "Where you headed for, boy?" Marion told him and the fellow gave him directions. Minutes later, Marion Michael was back clutching the feathered creatures by their legs and, on Ford's command, released them.

They flapped their wings and flew off to various parts of the set, some roosting under the eaves of houses, others simply waddling on the street.

After the scene was shot, Ford wanted the geese and ducks removed from the set. He called to Marion Michael.

"Hey, gooseherder," the director shouted, "get these birds the hell out of here!"

"You've got to picture that man Ford," said Wayne. "He was then and still is one of the few authentic geniuses in the motion picture business. He's huge and strong, mentally as well as physically. Outwardly, he's a tough, sarcastic character."

Marion Michael's ears flushed when Ford called him "gooseherder."

He stared at the director with anger frozen on his face.

Ford glared back at the hulking member of his "swing gang" and goaded him.

"You one of Howard Jones's bright boys?"

"Yes, Mr. Ford," Marion Michael replied.

"And you call yourself a football player?" Ford demanded.

"I don't . . . I mean . . . well . . ." Morrison stuttered.

"You're a guard, eh?" Ford pursued.

Wayne nodded.

"Let's see you get down in position," Ford commanded.

"I was tempted to throw a punch at Ford's jaw," Wayne recalls. "But I thought the better of it. I did as he asked. I kneeled down and braced my hands and feet against the ground . . ."

Ford walked over to the crouched Marion Michael, gave him the once-over, then kicked Marion's hands. The young football star collapsed on his face in the dirt.

"And you call yourself a guard?" Ford chuckled. "Why, I'll bet you couldn't even take *me* out!"

Marion Michael looked at the director for a long moment.

"I'd like to try," he finally said.

"You're on," Ford taunted and trotted down the field about twenty feet.

Marion charged after him.

"He tried to evade my charge but I lashed out with a leg," Wayne said. "I kicked him hard in the chest. He landed on the place he apparently thought football players carried their brains."

Ford glared at Marion Michael for a minute, then burst out laughing.

All at once Marion Michael Morrison had a job for life!

"That was the beginning of the most profound relationship of my life," Wayne said. "And, I have little doubt, the greatest friendship. Since that morning, John Ford directed me in several of my finest movies. I have hunted with him, fished with him, and shared many a bottle with him. I have played poker with him, and I've sought out his keen advice a thousand times. Were it not for my good friend John Ford's belief in me as an actor, I think I would still be playing cowboy sheriffs in third-rate Westerns."

After that unsportsmanlike kick, which had provoked

thunderous laughter from everyone on the set—including the star of *Mother Machree*, Victor McLaglen—John Ford assured Marion Michael of employment at the Fox Studios for all the rest of his summers away from USC.

This was the beginning for Marion Michael Morrison. He was destined to learn the movie business and to go on to stardom.

CHAPTER IV

His First Love,
His First Picture

By the time Marion Michael Morrison returned to the University of Southern California that fall of 1926, he was not only $500 richer but on the way toward his first romance. He didn't know it then, in September, but two months later it hit him like a fullback charging on his blind side.

It was November and Marion Michael, with some fraternity brothers, drove to a dance in Balboa, which in those days was years away from being overrun with sailors and marines. It was a simple, quiet fishing village.

Someone had fixed up Marion Michael with a blind date —a pretty, dark-eyed, dark-haired beauty from south of the border named Carmen Saenz. Her father was a Panamanian envoy serving in the consulate at Los Angeles. After an evening of conversation and dancing, Marion Michael took Carmen home.

But that wasn't the end. At Carmen's house the lights were still on, although it was well past midnight. Carmen's younger sister, Josephine, had returned home earlier and was entertaining her date in the living room. After Marion Michael and Carmen walked in, someone suggested, "Why don't we all go out and get a hamburger?"

That someone was Marion Michael Morrison.

They went to an all-night diner and after a while, as they were sitting in a booth talking, Marion Michael glanced suddenly into Josephine's eyes and it hit him.

"Chris' sake," he said to himself, "I'm in love with this girl."

For the first time in Marion Michael Morrison's life he was in love. He was nineteen years old and he was in love —irrevocably!

About an hour later, after excuses had been made, Marion Michael abandoned Carmen, took Josephine to the end of a pier, and sat near the edge of the pilings with her. He remembers staring out at the moonlit Pacific and feeling hypnotized by this girl. He put his arms around her, drew her close to him, and his lips met hers caressingly, first lightly, then urgently.

Marion Michael stiffened his embrace around Josephine and whispered to himself, "Wow! Tonight I am becoming a man . . ."

Marion Michael Morrison, who had come to USC from high school with a 94 average, continued to set that kind of academic pace in classes and made even more impressive strides on the football field.

In that fall semester at USC, Marion Michael Morrison knuckled down in his studies, striving to surpass the 85 average that his athletic scholarship required of him. In his freshman year he attained an 89 average, and in the first several weeks of his sophomore year he hovered again at that level.

But down on the football field, it was a different story. Marion Michael was having difficulty maneuvering across the yard stripes and found it impossible to throw a block or tackle. His right shoulder was throbbing with pain.

It had all begun at Balboa when Marion Michael discovered romance with Josephine. They had taken a dip in the ocean and in their youthful zest, Marion and Josephine raced over the beach and plunged headlong into the surf. They were met squarely by a high Pacific roller which tossed them far up on the beach. Josephine screamed with delight.

"Let's do it again!" she laughed.

But Marion Michael couldn't. He was doubled up in pain. His right shoulder ached something fierce. It felt better when Josephine rubbed it—but the pain didn't go away. Next day, Marion Michael went to the team doctor who examined the shoulder and diagnosed the injury as torn muscles and ligaments.

"My advice, son, is stay away from the football field," the doctor said. "It's going to take months for that shoulder to heal."

But Marion Michael was on a football scholarship. If he didn't play, he feared, the coach might just decide that Morrison was expendable and cancel that free ticket to an education. So he ignored the doctor's advice, went back on the field—and reinjured the shoulder on the first play from scrimmage in the game against that year's best Pacific Coast Conference team, Stanford, which was Rose Bowl-bound.

The following week, Marion Michael came out for practice, his shoulder now strapped in a special harness. It was no use. He couldn't stand the pain. The football season was over for Marion Michael.

In that crisis, he went to see John Ford, for whom Marion Michael had worked the previous summer as a "gooseherder." When the movie director saw the tall, neatly crewcut youth standing next to him on the Fox set, he gave him a wry grin.

"Got your ass kicked in last Saturday, didn't you?" he asked, referring to the USC-Stanford game.

"Hurt my shoulder," Marion Michael said. "I think I'm out for the season."

"Come over here," Ford said, leading Marion by the hand to a quiet corner of the set. "I know you have a football scholarship and all that," Ford began, "but I've got a little advice to give you. In fact, I'm strongly urging you to do it—quit school after this year . . ."

"I can't quit school!" Marion protested. "That's the most important thing to me. I'm thinking of becoming a lawyer . . ."

"I'm not saying quit altogether," Ford explained. "Just stay out of school a year. Give the shoulder a chance to heal."

"What'll I do meanwhile?" Marion wanted to know.

"What you did last summer . . . come and work for me," Ford said. "You come and see me as soon as school lets out. I'll find something for you to do like propping . . ."

There was a long pause and then Ford, looking Marion up and down, added, "Or maybe some acting, who knows?"

"Acting?" Marion exclaimed.

"Sure," Ford smiled, starting to walk back to his camera crew, "I've done wonders with worse slobs than you . . ."

That spring of 1927, Marion Michael packed his books and wardrobe into two suitcases, said goodbye to his teammates, his roomies, and his Sigma Chi friends, took one last disconsolate look around the dormitory, walked outside, glanced fondly at the huge, beautiful sprawl of the campus, and headed toward the exits.

It was a sad moment for him, for Marion Michael Morrison somehow had the strange sensation that he wasn't coming back—not after a year, not ever.

He had been bitten by the acting bug. John Ford hadn't promised anything, but the mere suggestion that he might let him act was all that Marion Michael needed to launch him into a private orbit of dreams.

"I thought about my days on Louise Street and the 'movies' I starred in," Wayne reminisced. "I had always wanted to act, I guess, but it never occurred to me when I was a kid that I'd ever get this close to it. Although the Triangle Studios were practically in my backyard, nobody in those days wanted to look at a kid with a dirty face and torn blue jeans. Becoming an actor then was only a wild dream and Hollywood was a city in some distant galaxy."

As he had promised, John Ford had a job waiting for Marion Morrison—as a prop man.

"How about acting, Mr. Ford?" the young man asked almost tremblingly.

"I didn't say for sure, I said maybe," Ford snapped. "Now don't bother me . . ."

For something like six months, Marion Michael Morrison toiled around the studio, lugging furniture like a moving man and jumping at every command barked by Ford and his many assistants. He felt like a laborer, which he was. And he would have quit after that half year in such an unrewarding job—if it had not been for a small handful of crumbs that John Ford finally tossed to him.

They were acting crumbs, brief but heartening moments before the cameras. Marion Michael's debut on 35mm film was in a Ford vehicle entitled *Hangman's House* on which shooting began in late January, 1928. It wasn't until something like the third week of production that Ford approached his tall, broad-shouldered "grip" and whispered:

"I have a part for you."

"In this picutre?" Marion almost choked.

The role didn't exactly make Marion Michael Morrison a star. In fact, when he went to see himself on the screen at a neighborhood movie theater, he had to look sharply not to miss his scene. He had been given the tiny role of a poor Irish boy brought before a judge. All Duke had to do was bow his head as the judge imposed sentence:

"You shall hang by the neck until dead, dead, dead!"

"I thought it was a pretty corny line," Wayne recalls. At the last rehearsal, after the judge had spoken the words, Marion was impelled to blurt out in what he thought was a whisper, "Amen!"

Ford let out a roar. "Get that idiot off this set! And never let me set eyes on him again!"

John Ford was later to say that it was at this moment he first realized there was something in Marion Michael that could project genuine emotion from a movie screen.

Even if his appearance on the screen lasted but a fleeting moment, Marion Michael Morrison was extremely proud of himself. For he had seen himself in a movie with three of the great stars of that era, the last days of silent pictures and the onrush of talkies. The stars of *Hangman's House* were Victor McLaglen, Hobart Bosworth, and June Collyer.

After *Hangman's House*, Marion Michael continued working as a grip and more months dragged by without an encouraging word from John Ford about another role. But in late April, 1929, Ford summoned Wayne to his office.

"I want you to do something for me, Duke," Ford said. Most of his coworkers around the studio were calling Marion by his nickname, and now the director was, too. Ford explained what he wanted: Go to the Trojan coach, Howard Jones, and beg him to let his team off from classes two weeks early.

"We're going to make a football picture and we're going to shoot a lot of it at Annapolis," Ford said. "I sent some guys over to the college to get the players off early but they wouldn't go for it. Now I'm asking you to try and talk them into it . . ."

Ford then tossed in this incentive:

"If you get me those players, I'll give you a good part in the picture."

Morrison went to see Jones but it was no sale.

"It's not I who won't let them get out of classes early," Jones protested. "It's the dean. He thinks they'll lose too much classroom work . . . and, besides, there are those final exams."

But Duke's persuasiveness finally prevailed. He convinced Jones, who convinced the academicians at USC, that the trip to Annapolis would be an education in itself for the players. Not only that, but they'd get to see Washington, D.C., and "maybe even visit President Herbert Hoover in the White House," not to mention the Penn Relays at the University of Pennsylvania in Philadelphia.

Salute, the film that resulted from this effort, by no means thrust Marion Michael Morrison into a spectacular rocketing of the cinematic heavens, but he received slightly greater exposure than in *Hangman's House*, for now he played the role of a football player. But even in this game he knew so well, he wasn't allowed to show his prowess on screen. George O'Brien was the hero of this football extravaganza, which was made in that sensational and revolutionary process that had caused such an upheaval in Hollywood—sound.

Movie fans may also be interested to learn that *Salute* also marked the debut of another extra who one day in the not too distant future would become a big name in Hollywood—Ward Bond—who played a role in the football sequences similar to Marion Michael's.

Even before *Salute* premiered in September, 1929, John Ford was gathering the cast for his next production, *Men Without Women*. Most of the filming was done off the Southern California coast, for it was a story about submarines. Young Morrison had gone on location as a prop man and happened to be standing near Ford as the director shouted orders to six professional stunt men.

They had been dressed as sailors for a scene in which it was supposed to look as if they'd been shot out of a torpedo tube. To create the effect of a churning air bubble, Ford had a huge high-pressure air hose submerged in the water. The stunt men-sailors were to dive into the water and come up at that point. The stunt had to be done just then because the destroyers in the distance were belching black smoke against a background of white clouds and blue sky—it was the perfect moment.

Ford gave the order. But the sea was heavy and the six stunt men chickened out.

"When they got a look at that water and the boats thrashing around out there they wanted no part of it," Ford recalled. "I was frantic. The sky, the smoke, everything was perfect at the moment. In a few minutes the whole setting would be changed. I looked around and saw Duke.

"Before I had a chance to finish asking him if he would give it a try, Duke dived into the water and came up in the air bubble . . . He not only did it once, he did it six times in a row—taking the places of all six stunt men. It took an awful lot of guts.

"So, I decided this fellow either has to be crazy, or he wanted to be an actor awfully bad."

Ford never forgot Marion Michael for saving the scene.

Of course, Ford saw to it that Marion Michael Morrison was listed in the credits—behind the film's stars, Kenneth MacKenna, Frank Albertson, and Paul Page. Then, after being rewarded with another bit part in *Rough Romance*, Marion Michael returned to his primary role at the Fox studios as a grip.

It was September, 1930, and classes at USC were starting.

Marion Michael thought about the talk he had had with John Ford, who had suggested he stay away from college a year. Three years had passed now and where was he in the film world, Morrison asked himself.

Wouldn't it be wiser to return to college, finish his remaining years, and pursue his original goal—law?

He decided to talk about it with Ford. But he didn't know how to approach the director. Every time he went near him, Ford growled at Duke. For days, he thought about the best way to seek Ford out and ask his advice.

Unknown to the Duke, however, John Ford was at that

very moment laying the groundwork for the birth of a new Hollywood superstar who would be known as John Wayne.

Ford had been talking to another of Fox's directing giants, Raoul Walsh, who was having problems casting for a major Western epic that would be called *The Big Trail*. He had rounded up most of the players but he had not been able to find a tall, rugged, true man-of-the-West type.

"I just won't settle for those pretty boys," Walsh told Ford. "And I don't want any of these Hollywood cowboys who have to stand on a box to make love to Marguerite Churchill. I want a real man."

"Why don't you come over to my lot?" Ford said.

"What have you got there that I haven't already seen?" Walsh asked.

"I want you to take a look at a young man who is propping for me," Ford explained. "I've had the kid in a few walk-on roles and he seems to *react* exceptionally well."

Walsh agreed to take a look. Ford didn't breathe a word of his talk with Walsh to Marion Michael. Next morning, April 17, 1930, Duke was back at the set working as a grip.

"Hey, Duke," someone shouted to him, "go and get those chairs for the scene." He left, picked up the chairs at the property department, and started back. As Marion Michael crossed a studio street, he spotted Ford talking with a man he did not recognize. The man had a black patch over his right eye. Marion Michael glanced at the man only for an instant. But it was enough to give him "a weird feeling." The man was staring at Marion with his good left eye.

After delivering the chairs for the interior set, Duke was told to get a table from the prop department. Back across the street he went. Ford was still talking to the stranger with the eyepatch, who was still eyeing Marion steadily.

On his return, the stranger's stare occupied Marion's mind so completely that he didn't see the lighting cable stretched across the street. He tripped over the cable and tumbled forward. The table fell to the pavement and broke into five pieces.

As Duke gathered up the pieces and took them back to the prop department for repairs, the man with the eyepatch watched, then turned to Ford.

"I like the way that kid walks . . . You know, I can't get that other kid whose walk I like so much, so maybe I'll take a flyer on this one . . ."

The other "kid" that director Raoul Walsh was referring to was Gary Cooper who, fresh from his starring triumph in *The Virginian*, was cast by Paramount in the French Foreign Legion epic called *Morocco*, costarring Marlene Dietrich. Even if Coop hadn't been tied down on a current film production, Paramount would never have entertained the idea of loaning out their rising young star to Fox—not for a minute.

About an hour after his trip to the prop department, Marion Morrison was approached by Eddie Grainger, one of Fox's assistant directors.

"Duke," Grainger said, "you'd better not take any more haircuts."

"Marion looked at Grainger with a puzzled expression.

"I'm not planning to be a musician, Eddie," Marion quipped, not quite certain what Grainger was leading up to.

"This is on the level, Duke," Grainger said. "Walsh likes

your looks. He may put you in a big Western he's getting ready to shoot. So you better let your hair grow long. I'm pretty sure he's going to screen-test you."

Morrison couldn't believe his ears. If this was some kind of a joke, he told himself, well . . . Grainger'd better get ready to duck.

It was no kidding, though, because two days later Walsh summoned Marion Michael to his office.

"You've been very highly recommended to me," Walsh said, "and I've decided to test you. But before I do that, I want you to learn to throw knives. Report to Steve Klemenko. He will teach you. You will be on regular salary. I've taken you off your prop job . . ."

What was Marion Michael Morrison's reaction at that moment?

Let John Wayne tell it the way he remembers it.

"I wish I could tell you my heart was pounding wildly at the prospect of becoming a movie star. It would not be true. It was just a job to me. And, besides, I figured what kind of goddamn starring role can this be if I've got to learn to throw knives?"

After two weeks, Morrison went to see Walsh.

"Now I know how to throw knives," he said.

"Good," Walsh snapped. "The next step is voice training and dramatics."

The avalanche called sound which had cascaded upon Hollywood in 1927 had by now revolutionized motion picture techniques. Hollywood imported voice and diction experts, drama coaches, and acting technicians by the trainload to teach movie actors how to talk. Among them were a few phonies.

"My teacher was one of those," Wayne recalled. "He had

me mincing on my toes, making sweeping gestures with my right arm, rolling my r's."

After six lessons, Duke told the teacher:

"I do not think I am getting anything out of these damn lessons. I think I ought to stop them."

"An excellent idea, sir," the teacher sighed. "And may I say that if you live to be a hundred years old, you will never become an actor."

This incident touched on something that has always bugged John Wayne. Many, many years ago, a reviewer quoted him as saying to his leading lady:

"Yer bee-ood-iful in yer wrath."

Wayne protested that he had never talked that way on-screen or off.

"Why, when I first started in movies," he said, "I had to learn how to say 'ain't' properly."

When Wayne saw those quotes in a magazine, and also another alleged spoken line attributed to him, "I take you *fer* wife," he blew his stack. He sat down and wrote to the magazine editor, pointing out his 94 average in school, including that same grade for English.

"I studied Latin and other languages as well," Wayne protested, "and took mathematics through calculus."

The truth of it, however, is known to many persons who recall Wayne as Genghis Khan in *The Conqueror* in 1956, for what he said to Tartar woman Susan Hayward in that film sounded very much like, "Yer bee-ood-iful in yer wrath." Even if John Wayne thinks otherwise. perhaps it was just a slip of the tongue, for . . .

Wayne, like college-bred Gary Cooper, may have impressed movie-goers over the years with a lack of articulation and excesses of mispronounciation, but these faults in all instances were deliberate, dictated by script and dialogue requirements. It wasn't that Duke, or Coop for that matter, had inadequate equipment for speaking the King's English. Both happen to have been excellent grammarians in school and, as the biographer of both men, I can attest that each went to college and achieved high grades in English.

In any case, after calling a halt to the lessons Morrison went back to Walsh, who was grinning.

"The coach tells me you will not be an actor in a hundred years," Walsh said.

"He's got something there," Duke admitted. "I guess I might as well go back to Ford and get my grip's job back," Morrison started to leave.

"Wait a minute!" Walsh ordered. "I'm going to test you tomorrow anyway."

CHAPTER V

A Star is Born—Almost

No one called Marion Michael Morrison by his first name anymore. He was known to everyone at the Fox studios as Big Duke. And when the big guy appeared for his screen test the morning after Raoul Walsh had stunned him, he was in for another surprise. There was no script and there were no lines to memorize. He was simply ordered to stand with Ian Keith and Marguerite Churchill, who already had been hired for *The Big Trail*.

They were taking part in Morrison's test beside a covered wagon.

"Now, Duke," Walsh called out, "you're the head scout. Your job is to lead this wagon train west. These people will ask you a lot of questions and you answer whatever comes into your mind."

Morrison looked at Walsh, who saw his puzzled expression.

"You heard me right," Walsh said. "And for Pete's sake don't try to act! Just be yourself. Natural."

As the cameras whirred, Keith fired questions at Duke.

"How long is this trip gonna be?"

"Where are we gonna eat?"

"Are we gonna see buffaloes?"

"Is there any danger of Indian attacks?"

Keith had studied the script and was well prepared with the dialogue of questions he triggered at Duke with machine gun rapidity. Morrison tried to give him answers . . .

"I was tripping all over my tongue," Wayne recalls. "I felt like a clumsy lout."

Suddenly Marion Michael began to burn. He did something he hadn't planned—he lost his temper. He started throwing angry, growling questions at Keith:

"Where ya from, mister?"

"Why do you want to go west?"

"Can you handle a rifle?"

Marion Michael wasn't acting. He was *reacting*—precisely what Walsh wanted him to do.

Now it was Keith's turn to look clumsy under the hammering barrage of Duke's impromptu questions. He stammered. He looked around confused.

"I had fixed him," Wayne said. "But I also figured, likewise myself. It relieved me to have gotten back at Keith, but it also frightened me. I said to myself, 'Goodbye acting career.'"

But Marion Michael Morrison had a big surprise coming.

"Cut!" yelled Walsh.

"Well, it's over for sure now," Duke said to himself, turning to look at the director. The dour expression on Walsh's face suddenly changed. His lips curled into a smile. Then he shouted the most beautiful words to a move actor's ears.

"Print it!"

It meant the scene was good.

A week later, John Ford summoned Marion.

"Pack your bags," he said. "You got the lead in *The Big Trail*. And good luck."

All at once, Marion Michael Morrison was a star! Not in just another pedestrian oater but a super-spectacle that was going to cost Fox an astronomical $3 million. The film was to be shot in a revolutionary wide-screen technique called Grandeur Process, similar to what the still undeveloped Cinemascope and Cinerama would be like years later. Grandeur required that theater stages be equipped with a new wide screen, while projectors needed special wide-angle lenses.

"Star!" Wayne exclaimed, as he recalled his first leading-man role. "They budgeted 3 million potatoes for that picture and do you know what my salary was? A miserable seventy-five dollars a week. What a laugh."

Many years later, Raoul Walsh was to be asked why he ever picked a prop man to be the star of *The Big Trail*.

"Because there was something about the hang of his shoulders, and that shuffle, that I thought I could use in the picture, and partly because I had to find somebody immediately. That wasn't the best picture I ever made, and the part wasn't too exacting. What I needed was a feeling of honesty, of sincerity—and Wayne had it."

Walsh stopped, scratched his head, adjusted his eye-patch, and went on.

"Wayne always had it and he will always have it. He has that unique quality of being able to underact. It's mighty effective. Not because he tries to underact—it's a hard thing to do, if you try—but because he can't overact.

"The trouble with most competent but ungifted actors, and that's what the Duke is, is that they think they're wonderful. Wayne does not. Why, I used to have the devil of a time with him. He'd read a script and shake his head. 'I can't do the part that way,' he'd say. 'It's too hard. I'm not good enough for it.' It's the attitude he has about himself which makes him so *right* for every picture he plays in."

After the shooting of *The Big Trail* was finished and the last rushes were taken to the viewing room, the art department brought in its can of film bearing the picture's titles. Among those watching the screen that afternoon was Winfield Sheehan, head of production at Fox. When he caught sight of the name Marion Michael Morrison in the leading trailer, he leaped out of his seat.

"What kind of a name is that for a dauntless he-man of the early West!" he roared. "We can't let that get out to the public. They'll laugh us right out of every theater."

Next morning, Sheehan called Duke to his office.

"That name of yours," he said, "it's gotta go. We can't work with it. It's the wrong label."

"What's wrong with my name?" Wayne asked. "Had it all my life. Proud of it, too."

"You don't look like a Marion Michael Morrison," Sheehan said.

"What do I look like?" Duke wanted to know.

"You look like a John Wayne," Sheehan replied. "And that's who you're going to be from now on—John Wayne!"

The Big Trail launched John Wayne on a perpendicular ride that was to survive for an incredible four decades and more—right to the present day. Yet by all standards that Hollywood had established in those days and which still exist in that city today, Wayne should have been out of the ball game after that first starring role.

Because the picture was a flop.

It wasn't so much that the picture was all that bad or that Wayne's performance left a great deal to be desired; it had more to do with the times. The film, released in November, 1930, came out practically on the first anniversary of the 1929 Wall Street Crash. This was the era of the Great Depression. People were selling apples on streetcorners, and the poverty which had descended on the country took a terrible toll at the box offices.

Moreover, showing the film had unique requirements— the Grandeur Screen and wide-angle projector lenses—and few independent theater managers or chain movie houses wanted to put money into a process that, as events proved, was twenty-five years ahead of its time. As Wayne summed it up:

"*The Big Trail* laid a very impressive egg."

Not until a quarter century later, when Cinemascope came into its own, was the wide-screen technique introduced by the pioneering Raoul Walsh ever tried again. And then, the very cameras with which Walsh filmed his 1930 Western epic were dragged out of mothballs and cranked up to shoot Cinemascope's spectacular extravaganza *The Robe*.

When it became apparent that few theaters would show *The Big Trail* in the 70mm Grandeur process, Fox put out a conventional 35mm film. But even this one didn't make many ripples at the box office.

Although reviewers hardly raved about John Wayne, his

usefulness to Fox was not entirely destroyed by *Big Trail's* dismal showing. The film had a curiosity appeal because of its innovative wide-screen process and Wayne, as the star of the picture, was receiving some attention in newspapers around the country. Nothing spectacular, but at least his name was publicized.

Another Fox director, Seymour Felix, decided to team Duke again with his costar in *Big Trail*, Marguerite Churchill, in a thing called *Girls Demand Excitement.*

"That was the worst motion picture in the history of the industry," Wayne recalled.

It was filmed in a few short weeks on the Fox lot during December, 1930, and January, 1931, and there were no rugged mountain ranges, no meandering plains, no prickly cactus in the background. Wayne didn't have to head off anyone at the pass in this hour-long drag. The setting was a college campus. Duke turned into the wardrobe department the scout's duds he'd worn in *Big Trail* and was issued a passel of civilian suits—and a basketball uniform.

"Boy, did I hate making that picture," Wayne complained. "Damn, it was the most incredible plot. The high point was a basketball game between a boys' and girls' team. But even worse, there was that unbelievable dance director. Everything he did was by the count—one, two, three, four—and then your line. I was completely embarrassed."

Wayne found himself walking down the street talking to himself after one particularly exasperating day at the studio. Will Rogers, whom Duke had met by now, passed by. Wayne didn't even see him.

"Hey, Duke," Rogers called after him, "what's the matter?"

Wayne started to tell him.

Rogers smiled, patted him on the back, and said, "Well, you're workin', ain't ya?"

"Yeah, I guess I am," Wayne replied.

"That's the important thing," Rogers said. "So get at it and quit gripin'."

It was an admirable philosophy and one to which John Wayne clung from that day forward—just as he always stuck to his father's three fundamentals of living.

Even before the disaster that was *Girls Demand Excitement* could be recorded at the nation's box offices, Fox shoved John Wayne into another bomb entitled *3 Girls Lost*.

The only saving feature of this film was the presence of the lovely Loretta Young. But even Miss Young could't pull the picture up by its bootstraps. It wasn't a Western, thus there were no bootstraps to pull. Another flop.

So far as Fox was concerned, John Wayne was finished. Since he had no contract, the studio could stop his salary —all seventy-five dollars of it—just like that. And it did. He was an unemployed actor—for exactly one week.

No one at Columbia Studios has ever revealed what attracted them to John Wayne, but they did hire him and did immerse him in three quickie films: *Men Are Like That* (later renamed *Arizona*), *Range Feud*, and *Maker of Men*.

Wayne's tenure at Columbia was not a happy one. His run-in with that most tyrannical, most despised despot of Hollywood, Harry Cohn, the grand mahatma of Columbia Pictures, was the sorriest experience of his still brief career in the movie capital.

"The son of a bitch called me in one day and told me to lay off the bottle and broads," Wayne recalled. "I asked him what the hell he meant and he said he had documented evidence that I'd been boozing it up on the set and making eyes off-camera at one of the leading ladies."

Rumors were circulating around the studio that Wayne was engaged in a flirtation with the sultry Susan Fleming, who had starred with him in *Range Feud*. Whether true or not, the fact remains that Big John's main romantic interest was still the girl who won his heart that night on the dock at Balboa—Josephine Saenz.

By now, Duke and Josie were engaged and were talking about setting a wedding date—until Columbia gave him the bounce. It came on Christmas Eve of 1931, the very day that his last vehicle for Columbia, *Maker of Men*, was released to theaters around the country.

"Well, Josie," Wayne told his fiancée after breaking the bad news to her on Christmas Day, "at least I've got tickets for the Rose Bowl Game." A week later, on New Year's Day, Duke took his girl to the game and they cheered the mighty Trojan team to its second-in-a-row Tournament of Roses conquest, a lopsided victory over the Black Panthers of Pittsburgh, 35–0.

None of the USC players in this game had played with Duke in the years he was on the team, in 1925 and 1926. But there was always a tinge of sadness in Wayne's heart for having missed out on his last two years at USC. For had he returned after the layoff suggested by John Ford, Duke might have played in the 1930 Rose Bowl when the Trojans then, too, encountered Pittsburgh and skunked them 47–14.

Marion Michael Morrison, now better known as John Wayne, was still not too old to return to college, pick up his football career, and perhaps play in the Rose Bowl the following New Year's Day or the one after that, and conceivably he could even go on and become a lawyer as he had wanted. He was still only twenty-three years old.

He might have done just that had it not been for a phone call from Sid Rogell, head of Mascot Productions, one of the studios along Poverty Row, where low-budget quickie films were being ground out at a phenomenal one-a-day clip.

"We're going to shoot *Shadow of the Eagle*," Rogell told Wayne, "and we'd like you to be our star. Can you do it?"

There was a long stretch of silence.

"Did you hear me, Duke?" Rogell asked. "You're not saying anything."

Wayne was so overcome by the offer that he had lost his voice.

"Yes, I heard you," he finally managed to say. "You're damn right that I can do it."

Several days passed and Rogell phoned again. He wanted some personal data on Wayne.

"Are you a drinking man?" Rogell wanted to know.

"Of course, I am," Wayne replied. "I can drink with the best of 'em."

"How much do you drink on movie sets?" asked Mascot's prexy.

"On the sets?" Wayne was baffled. "Why, I don't drink anything but water and coffee when I'm shooting . . ."

Suddenly he realized what Rogell was leading up to. "That dirty son of a bitch, Harry Cohn, has been bad-mouthin' me aroun' town," Duke said to himself. He was sure of it when Rogell asked him another leading question:

"You don't screw around with your leading ladies, do you?"

"No, goddamn it!" Wayne thundered. "And if you

wanna tell me who's been spreadin' those lies about me I'll be happy to go down there and rip off Harry Cohn's balls —and cement them in the lobby of Grauman's Chinese."

A few days later, Rogell called Wayne again.

"Come on in," he said. "I've got a contract for you."

No one told Wayne what kind of a production *Shadow of the Eagle* was until director Ford Beebe handed him the script. It weighed a ton. Because this was a Western serial, twelve chapters long.

Wayne didn't mind. He was working again. What he didn't know when he signed the contract with Mascot was that this was the beginning of a career as a horse-opera Hamlet that was to last a long seven years, during which he would grind out no fewer than fifty-two low-budget quickie Westerns, each with the same unchanging head-'em-off-at-the-pass plot, each bringing him nothing but a miniscule salary, each adding hardly anything to his reputation as an actor.

A month after John Wayne finished *Shadow of the Eagle*, he became intimately acquainted with the unvaryingly incomprehensible, topsy-turvy logic of Hollywood. With early reports following the release of *Eagle* indicating brisk business at the box office, Harry Cohn—his scruples always deferred to his materialism—decided John Wayne might not be a bad bet for another Columbia Western, and if he still suspected that Duke drank on the set and seduced his leading ladies in their dressing rooms, so what? What's a little alcohol and promiscuity off-camera if the picture makes money, Cohn is certain to have told himself.

The vehicle for Wayne this time was *Texas Cyclone*, and the only contributing force that raised this clod above most run-of-the-mill Poverty Row productions was the casting of

Walter Brennan in an exceptionally strong supporting role.

Cohn was so pleased with the results that he asked D. Ross Lederman, who directed *Texas Cyclone*, to handle the chores on *Two-Fisted Law*, which also starred Duke Wayne.

In the next twelve months, John Wayne churned out thirteen more films for five different studios. Count them: *Lady and Gent* in June, 1932, for Paramount; *Hurricane Express*, in the first part of July, for Mascot; *Ride Him Cowboy*, in the latter part of July, for Warner Brothers; *The Big Stampede*, in August, also for Warners; *Haunted Gold*, in October, once more for Warners; and again for Warners in December, *The Telegraph Trail*. In January, 1933, it was *The Three Musketeers*, another twelve-part serial, for Mascot, followed the month after with *Central Airport* for First-National, the first picture to bring John Wayne a measure of critical acclaim. This occurred for two reasons. He was directed by the great William A. Wellman, who had helped Gary Cooper to stardom in the memorable 1927 Paramount production of *Wings*. And he was costarred with the great Richard Barthelmess and had a strong supporting cast that included Sally Eilers and Tom Brown.

This film also saw John Wayne sans cowboy clothes for the first time since the celluloid debacle called *Girls Demand Excitement*.

Somewhere in Sonora came next, in April in 1933, for Warner Brothers; *The Life of Jimmy Dolan* followed in May for Warners again; and in June, *His Private Secretary*, for Showman's Pictures. Later that month, Wayne stepped up into some classy company when he teamed with Barbara Stanwyck, George Brent, and Donald Cook in Warner Brothers' *Baby Face*. A few weeks later, Warners put him into another Western, *The Man From Monterey*.

Thirteen pictures in one year! John Wayne was still not one of the celebrated stars of Hollywood—but he certainly was the hardest-working of them all. No one had set such a blistering pace as a leading man in all the history of the film citadel.

Did all this work make John Wayne rich?

At $150 a week, you can be sure it didn't. But it made him cognizant of one thing—he was heeled well enough to afford marriage.

"How about it," he said to Josie after the last scene of *Man From Monterey* was filmed, "shall we get married?"

"I thought you'd never ask," she trilled, threw her arms around Big Duke, and allowed herself to have a good cry.

CHAPTER VI

Stagecoach to Stardom

The marriage of John Wayne and Josie Saenz was an amalgamation of two people from opposite poles of the social spectrum. Wayne was just plain Duke, a movie actor of as yet little renown. Josephine's society was the real thing—strictly Pasadena, not Hollywood—and her crowd was an upper-stratum circle of cognoscenti who frequented the many social functions at the Panamanian Consulate in Los Angeles, where her father served as that Central American country's principal envoy.

To John Wayne, all things had come the hard way. Josephine had had everything handed to her on a silver platter. But they had one thing in common—love.

Though she had grown somewhat accustomed to Duke's seemingly incongruous movie career—most of all the long

64

hours, the exhausting work, and the small compensation—Josie Wayne apparently was determined to make her husband over in her own particular mold. But not at the beginning of their marriage.

After a brief honeymoon, John Wayne went back to work and now found himself very much in demand at Monogram Pictures, which signed him to a long-term contract at a salary that, as Wayne will attest, was not nearly commensurate with his ability. Nor was it a true mirror of the cataract of profits pouring into the film company's coffers from Duke's Western opuses.

But the promise made to Wayne by Trem Carr, production head at Monogram, gave him hope.

"I know you're mighty bored of being tied to railroad tracks and finding yourself in strange rooms where the walls contract and threaten to squeeze you to death at the end of a chapter," Carr said. "So I'm taking you out of the cobra pits. I'm going to make you a real Western star."

Riders of Destiny was Wayne's first picture for Monogram. It cost $11,000 to make—and that included everything.

The film was shot in what is commonly referred to as a "one-horse town"—and they weren't kidding!

"The budget was so tight we couldn't afford more than one horse," Wayne laughed. "So in the first scene I had to knock out the heavy and steal his horse, which he stole from the heroine's brother in the first place."

Just when John Wayne thought he was going to plunge into a second production for Monogram, he found himself out on loan to Warners once more for a football saga called *College Coach*, which costarred Dick

Powell, Pat O'Brien, and Ann Dvorak. Again William Wellman directed this celluloid tale of gridiron heroics. Wayne received mildly laudatory reviews.

Back on the Monogram lot, Duke Wayne was about to begin his longest run of movie productions for the same film-maker—a total of fifteen Western potboilers that would take him deep into 1935.

It was during the first of these cowboy sagas, *Sagebrush Trail*, that Wayne met one of filmland's most spectacular stunt men and rodeo riders, Yakima Canutt, who also had a featured role in the film.

Canutt, who had come to Hollywood in 1923 out of Colfax, Washington, and was eleven years older than Wayne, taught the Duke all his tricks, including how to fall from a galloping horse without getting hurt, the art of barroom brawling, and the right way to whip a gun out of its holster and shoot.

"I even copied Yak's smooth-rollin' walk," Wayne said without any reservation. "And the way he talks, kinda low and with quiet strength."

After *Sagebrush Trail* came *The Lucky Texan, West of the Divide, Blue Steel, The Man from Utah, Randy Rides Alone, The Star Packer, The Trail Beyond, The Lawless Frontier, 'Neath Arizona Skies, Texas Terror, Rainbow Valley, The Desert Trail, The Dawn Rider,* and *Paradise Canyon.*

It was now mid-1935, John Wayne had finished his forty-fifth film—and he was still nowhere in the movie firmament. A hack on horseback is what he really was. Yet this husky, loosely hinged guy with the lopsided grin and beamy shoulders, had in his own quiet way brought to Hollywood movie-making an acting technique that was as drastic as Raoul Walsh's 70mm Grandeur Screen process.

As he reflected upon the change he wrought during his dismal days as a cinematic cowboy, Wayne said:

"When I came in, the Western man never lost his white hat [Tom Mix] and always rode the white horse [Tom Mix] and waited for the man to get up again in the fight [Tom Mix]. Following my dad's advice, if a guy hit me with a vase, I'd hit him with a chair. That's the way we played it. I changed the saintly boy scout of the original cowboy hero into a more normal kind of fella."

Duke Wayne carried this concept out every time he went before the cameras at Monogram. Having become their top money-maker, he consequently held increasingly to the postulation that he could impose his own concepts concerning techniques employed in filming his Westerns.

"During a frontier saloon fight scene, I complained bitterly to the director about the action," Wayne explained. "Here they were, all those extras standing at the bar and this guy fires a shot right across their faces—and they're still standing there."

"Tell them to move their asses the hell outa there," Wayne said he told the director. "The trick is to get all that violence in motion. If you capture it here on film, you sure as hell are gonna release it in the neighborhood theater. Otherwise the picture's gonna bomb."

Don't get the idea that Wayne was a complainer. He wasn't. At least the work they gave him to do never bothered him. The few times he did open his yap to directors or producers, his action was prompted by the deep feelings he harbored for "artistic perfection" in films, even if they were nothing more than prosaic horse oprys. Duke had a sense of pride in his work.

Though John Wayne seldom griped about the back-breaking movie-making pace he had to maintain, back at home someone was complaining increasingly more loudly and bitterly. Josie Wayne was becoming disenchanted with her husband's deep commitment to his profession and she often didn't hesitate to tell him so.

Yet at the same time, it seemed, it made little difference to Josie that Duke had to report to the studio at 6:00 A.M. and spend a grueling day doing all his range and saloon fighting himself—there were no doubles in those days for him—as well as all the other action stuff required on a Western set. When he'd drag himself home dirty and tired at the end of the day, usually around 7:30 P.M., Wayne would stumble into the bedroom only to find that Josephine had laid out his dinner clothes on the bed.

And off he'd have to go to some party.

Speaking of the social excursions that he was compelled to make in those days, Wayne commented:

"A guy in pictures has got to look wide-eyed. I used to be so sleepy I could die. I loved having my friends around, but the routine of getting in at one in the morning and then up again at five to be on a horse in front of a camera at six —well, I began to curl up."

To Duke Wayne, only his *old* friends mattered to him— the people he had gone to school with and those few in the movie capital who became his lifelong confidants. By now two of his closest chums were Ward Bond and John Ford, and Wayne would have them over to the house as often as Josie allowed, which wasn't too often. She preferred to drag her Big Duke out to mingle with her society friends.

Despite the fact that he didn't give a tinker's damn for the *haute monde* of Josie's fashionable circle, Wayne loved every other aspect of life with his wife. They shared the same religious beliefs—they were both Roman Catholics—and they had strong feelings about children and family.

Indeed, the one major discordance in their early years of marriage, precipitated by Josie's predisposition to socialize, came to a somewhat abrupt end when she bore her husband their first child, a son named Michael, in 1934. Now all at once Josie was tied to the nursery, and this brought a temporary respite to the couple's nighttime perambulations.

Michael's birth was like a shot of adrenalin in Duke Wayne's heart. He worked more strenuously than ever before. He spent longer hours at the studio—and longer periods away from home because his assignments involved increasingly more numerous trips to far-off locations.

John Wayne suddenly found himself working for Republic Pictures, which had been shaped by a merger of Mascot, Monogram, Lone Star, and Consolidated, all prosaic Poverty Row Western film producers. His pact with Monogram made him a sort of chattel of the new conglomerate, but he didn't regret the arrangement since the new company had a far bigger financial structure than any other film producer he had worked for since Fox, Columbia, and Warners.

The genius behind the new combine called Republic was Herbert Yates, who himself had been a maker of undistinguished films until he lassoed the several straggly Poverty Row production companies under one roof. And Yates was ready to prove to Duke Wayne that Republic was going to be no piker when it came to investing in his pictures.

Yates plunged all of $17,000 (less than the salary Tom Mix used to get in a week) into Duke's first production for Republic, *Westward Ho!* The film was shot in less than three weeks and when it was released in August, 1935, reviewers across the land paid attention to it—and its rangy cowboy star.

By years's end, when box office returns were counted, *Westward Ho!* had grossed more than $500,000!

As Wayne put it, "It was a thirty to one payoff."

With profits like that, Republic could well afford to listen to the Big Duke when he had a suggestion here, a suggestion there. But director Robert N. Bradbury, who ran herd on *Westward Ho!* and Carl Pierson, who directed Wayne's next Western for Republic, *The New Frontier*, wouldn't listen when John asked them to put Yakima Canutt into the pictures. They had their own preference in actors and actresses for their pictures and Canutt wasn't one of them.

Bradbury also had ideas of his own. He wanted Wayne to play the role of Singing Sandy and/or Singing Sam. The director actually asked Duke to sing, or as Wayne recalled it:

"He wanted the he-ro to hummmmmmm. This hero of the West hummmmmmmed when he got mad, you know, 'Huh, duh-duh, duh-duh, dee-dum . . . guns will be blazin', guns will be blazin'. . . . hugh, duh-duh, duh-duh . . . with hate in your eyes . . . huh, duh-duh, duh-duh, dee-dum.'

"Now, I could get through that hummin' crap through one picture but I wasn't aimin' to make singing a career. But down South they liked the friggin' thing, so for the next film they told Bradbury to put in another song. Well, Bradbury really took that assignment to heart. He got lost in his direction and started spending more time writing songs instead of finding places for me to belt the heavies . . ."

Bradbury was the father of Bob Steele, who had played in many westerns and was one of the "Three Mesquiteers" after Wayne left the scenes. The director had another son attending USC.

"So Bradbury was going to make a singer out of me because he wanted to put his kid through college," Wayne went on. "I said bullshit but I went along with the gag for a little bit. And there's Bradbury's kid sittin' off the set with a guy who's playin' the banjo or harp or whatever—a geetar —and I sit in front of the camera and mouthing all this crap and phony-fingering a geetar.

"Well, they come along with the next picture and they want another song. They finally got up to four songs in one picture and before you know it they had me going on public appearances and over the top of my horse crappin' on the stage, everybody's screaming, 'Sing, sing, sing!'

"Well, I finally went to Ol' Man Yates and says, 'I've had it. I'm a goddamn action star, you son of a bitch. I'm not a singer. Go get yourself a singer!' "

And Yates did. He got Gene Autry, who became the first multimillionaire singin' cowboy.

Wayne was still very far from his first million at this time. With his emancipation from singing roles, he was told to report to Scott Pembroke, who was going to direct the Duke's next Western, *The Oregon Trail.* And this time, Yakima Canutt, whom John respected and loved—and co-pied—so well, was right up there in the cast, along with Ann Rutherford, the pretty dark-haired teenage starlet who one day in the not-too-distant future would be appearing with Mickey Rooney in the unforgettable Andy Hardy series.

Oregon Trail was the first of eight pictures that Duke Wayne made in 1936, a year which was memorable for him not so much because of his undiminished work in films but for two other exceptional reasons.

One was the birth of the Waynes' second child, a seven and one-half pound doll they named Antonia Maria but who would henceforth be called Toni.

The other had to do with a promise John Ford made to John Wayne. It had all started one summer's day when Ford was sailing off Catalina and came across an Ernest Haycox short story in *Collier's* magazine called "The Stage to Lordsburg." The role of the Ringo Kid, the story's hero, he told himself, could be played by only one person—Duke Wayne. The plot concerned the journey of a stagecoach through Indian-infested territory, which wasn't much above the cut of most run-of-the-mill Westerns. Yet there was something about the tale that grabbed Ford and gave him ideas.

Several nights later, Ford invited himself with Ward Bond over to Wayne's house for poker. Along about midnight when the cards were cleared off the table and they were hoisting bourbons and Scotches, Ford turned to Wayne and said:

"Duke, I've just bought a fine Western story which I had written into a film version I'm going to call *Stagecoach*." Ford reached into his leather case and pulled out the script.

"Read it for me, will you?" he said. "I can't think of an actor in town who can play the Ringo Kid."

Wayne read the story and told Ford he thought the only actor in Hollywood who could do it was Lloyd Nolan.

Ford glared at Wayne for what seemed an interminable period. Finally he thundered:

"Are you an idiot?" Couldn't you play it?"

Wayne was delighted that Ford wanted him for the role, for if he could do *Stagecoach* it would mean working for a major studio and reprieve, even emancipation, from the rat race of Poverty Row.

As the weeks and months, indeed the years passed, John Ford searched for a producer for his "baby." *Stagecoach* had become an obsession with Jack. He wanted more than anything else to bring it to the screen—but not without Wayne.

He found many producers willing to go for the picture—but not with John Wayne in the lead.

"Get another actor," Ford was told. "Get a big star.
Make *Stagecoach* with somebody else. That Wayne is a
third-rater . . ."

But Jack Ford stuck to his guns and obstinately
refused to make the picture without Duke.

So Wayne continued to toil in grade-B Westerns. In
the first half of 1936, Duke starred in five more sagebrush sagas for Republic—*Lawless Range, The Lawless
Nineties, King of the Pecos, The Lonely Trail,* and *Winds of the
Wasteland*—even before June had dawned on the calen-
dar.

Was he complaining?

Not at all. The salary was much improved over that
seventy-five dollars a week that Ford had paid him for
his first walk-on part in *Hangman's House.* Now eight
years later and after something already exceeding fifty
film titles to his credit, John Wayne had ambled along
with a constantly rising salary scale. He'd worked his
way up at Republic to $4,000 a picture, and when you
consider that it took three weeks to shoot those four
and five-reelers, he wasn't doing badly financially. Yet
his salary was far from the $7,500 a week that estab-
lished stars like Clark Gable and Gary Cooper were pulling down in that era.

But, then, Wayne wasn't yet in Gable's or Coop's
class. That very midsummer of 1936 when Duke com-
pleted his fifty-first film, *Winds of the Wasteland,* costarring Phyllis Fraser, Yakima Canutt, and Douglas Cos-
grove, Gary Cooper was having nearly simultaneous

world premieres of two of his films in New York City—
Desire at the Paramount Theater and the unforgettable *Mr.
Deeds Goes to Town* at Radio City Music Hall.

John Duke Wayne was still brushing the Western prairie
dust from his cowboy duds and nursing the bruises and
sprains suffered in his prodigious pratfalls. But the day of
reckonin' would come for Big Duke, too—although now
was not yet the time.

The breaks in film-making came slowly to John Wayne,
yet they came. As they did that day in May, 1936, when
Universal Pictures proffered him an eight-picture deal
which not only carried a salary of $6,000 a picture but also
a chance to hang up his chaps and spurs. They wanted him
to do non-Western action films. Duke leaped at the offer.

His first venture in this new field was *The Sea Spoilers*, a
tale about the briny deep, and it was followed in quick
succession by such horseless epics as *Conflict, California
Straight Ahead, I Cover the War, Idol of the Crowds*, and *Adventure's End*.

This skein of films took Wayne deep into 1937 and by
now Josie informed him that they were expecting another
delivery from the stork. Duke still had a commitment to do
one more non-Western production for Universal, but he
asked for a reprieve. He felt his new roles were disenfran-
chising him from the fans who were his followers along the
dusty trails of Coyote Gulch and Varmint Valley.

He grabbed his saddle and headed for the Paramount lot
where Gary Cooper, at six feet two and a half inches still
loomed a head taller than the six-foot four Duke, but it was
a chance that Wayne had been waiting for. He was teamed
with Charles Barton, Marsha Hunt, James Craig, and
Johnny Mack Brown in a sagebrush adventure entitled *Born*

to the West, which not only rekindled his popularity among the faithful John Wayne Western fans but also gave him a great deal of exposure. Paramount's film distribution was far wider in range and scope than Universal's, and the outlets that B. P. Schulberg had in those days were the very best theaters in the country.

Even as he finished work on *Born to the West*, Wayne had an additional reason to rejoice—Josie had given birth to another chip off the old block, an eight-pound strapling named Patrick.

Yet even now as parents of three children, those early differences that Duke and Josie experienced continued to grate them. The enforced separations precipitated by Wayne's location work and his wife's insistence on traveling in her preferred and more familiar upper-crust circles kept the undercurrent of disharmony coursing constantly through their marriage.

The joy of birth in 1938 was accompanied by the sorrow of death. Doc Morrison died of a heart attack.

While Paramount was pleased with Wayne's services, they didn't dangle any contract in front of his face. So it was back to the salt mines for Duke. Republic saddled him up on four more bing-bing-bing, bang-bang-bang Western gallops—*Pals of the Saddle, Overland Stage Raiders, Santa Fe Stampede,* and *Red River Range.*

The year 1938 was rapidly drawing to a close. John Wayne was celebrating ten years in movies during which he had made sixty-two pictures, and what did he have to show for it, really? He was still a clod in the eyes of many moviegoers, and certainly the big producers of Hollywood knew that even better than the people who kept the box office registers ringing.

Well, at least there was something for Wayne to look forward to—he had his three kids to see each time he walked through the front door, and nothing in the world made him happier. He didn't care that much about glittering success, so long as those kids were healthy and happy. He was earning more than enough to provide them with all the earthly goods that they could want. They were a hell of a lot better off than he had been at their stages of life.

Besides, it was New Year's Day and not since 1933, when Southern California had polished off Pittsburgh by that 35–0 score, had the Trojans played in the Rose Bowl. But now they were back, on this first day of 1939, and Duke and Josie rooted for them lustily with the other 99,099 fans to a hairbreadth 7–3 victory over the powerful and highly-favored Blue Devils of Duke University.

That wasn't all that John Wayne had to cheer about.

"Duke, I've got some good news," the voice on the other end of the phone said.

"What'd you do, beat Ward in poker?" Wayne chided.

"Listen to me, you big bum . . . I've gotten a producer for *Stagecoach* . . ."

Duke had a lump in his throat. He swallowed hard. His mind was a Greek salad—a thousand thoughts were racing through it but only one was clear. He remembered the script Jack Ford had given him to read. He remembered recommending Lloyd Nolan for the Ringo Kid. He also had not forgotten that no producer would let Ford do the picture with an actor of Wayne's mediocrity. Did Lloyd Nolan get the part, he wondered? He didn't dare ask.

"Wh . . . why . . . why ya . . . ya . . . callin' me?" he stammered.

"Because, you son of a bitch," Ford bellowed, "you're going to be the Ringo Kid!"

CHAPTER VII

Exit Josie, Enter Chata

Walter Wanger was always a sucker for ideas—if they were good ones. The movie capital's leading independent producer had listened to John Ford's outline of *Stagecoach* with intense interest. Jack promised him this wasn't going to be another of those gallop-gallop-gallop Westerns but something unique and unforgettable. There was going to be deep characterization, careful dialogue, painstaking direction, superb photography, all the authentic atmosphere of a fine, top-flight picture. Yet it would still be a Western.

"And who do you propose for the Ringo Kid's part?" Wanger wanted to know.

"There's only one man who can play that role," Ford said, almost afraid to mention the name.

"Gary Cooper, of course," Wanger smiled. "But you may

have a little trouble lining him up . . . he's got a few other commitments, you know."

Ford took a deep breath.

"I wasn't thinking of Coop," the director said.

"No, then who?" the man with the money bags wanted to know.

"I won't have anyone but John Wayne play the Ringo Kid," Ford said with a firmness that convinced Wanger that he meant it and that his position was irreversible.

"Well, you recommended Wayne to Raoul [Walsh] for *The Big Trail*," Wanger said, "and you know what happened then. But that was ten years ago. I guess a man is entitled to goof once every decade . . ."

Ford and Wanger then put their heads together and came up with the rest of the cast—Claire Trevor, to play the kind-hearted trollop; Thomas Mitchell, the boozing doctor; George Bancroft, the leathery skinned sheriff; John Carradine, the ostracized gambler; and Andy Devine, the kooky stagecoach whip.

As Wayne now looks back on that period of his life, he recalls some things that he can comment on—in retrospect.

"Now that *Stagecoach* has become a classic, it is easy to say it was obvious that I was the ideal Ringo Kid," Wayne said. "But in those days it was far from obvious. Everybody told Ford he was committing suicide, risking a third-rate bum like me in a million-dollar production."

Well, at least Ford wasn't gambling as much as Walsh did when he put Wayne in *The Big Trail*—a $3 million bet that paid off with the noise of a crash as deafening as the stock market collapse of 1929.

Not for a moment did Jack Ford have any doubts that Wayne would make good as the Ringo Kid and that *Stage-*

coach would be one of the greatest Westerns of all time. Yet you wouldn't have thought Ford had any such notions when filming got under way in early 1939 at the United Artists studios.

It was his first day before the cameras. Duke Wayne, playing the Ringo kid, a tough youngster who really is decent at heart, has been accused of shooting his father to death. He breaks out of jail in pursuit of the real killers. In his opening scene, he enters the stagecoach and the passengers ask him who he is.

"The Ringo Kid. That's what my friends call me. But my right name's Henry."

These three sentences were John Wayne's passport to fame—but you'd never have guessed it if you were on the set that morning.

"Don't you know how to walk?" Ford screamed at Duke. "You're as clumsy as a hippo . . . And stop slurring your dialogue and show some expression. You look like a poached egg!"

All that day and the next, Ford gave Wayne the worst ragging of his career. But on the third day, Ford nudged the big fellow and whispered, "Don't worry, Duke . . . you're good. Damn good."

"Years later," Wayne now smiles, "Jack explained why he had deliberately bullied me. He had two reasons. First, he knew if he could arouse my anger, it would mobilize all my emotions and I would give a better performance. He wanted to help me shake off the bad habits of ten years of mechanical acting in those quickie Westerns.

"Secondly, he was afraid the other actors, who were all big stars, would resent the fact that Ford had placed one of his proteges in an important role. By taking the offensive against me, Ford suspected he could get the rest of the cast on my side. His tactics worked beautifully."

Stagecoach was an instant success. It became a classic of the genre. And John Wayne, who had been plodding on the treadmill of grade-B Westerns and drab adventure yarns for his first ten years in Hollywood, was catapulted overnight to archetype casting.

Following the wagon tracks of *Stagecoach*, Duke became "the essential Western man," as *Time* put it so succinctly not long ago, "fearin' God but no one else. Tough to men and kind to wimmin, slow to anger but duck behind the bar when he got mad, for he had a gun and a word that never failed."

But as John Wayne put it years before the national weekly awakened to him and tossed him its tributes:

"A man pays a high price for success, particularly in Hollywood. He surrenders his private life and often his happiness. I sometimes wonder if I would have been better off if I had remained the easy-going, never-care-for-tomorrow fellow I was when I started. But somewhere along the line I changed. Maybe it was getting married and having children that changed me, filled me with an urge to prosper and provide a better life and economic security for my family . . ."

We're going to come to that *high price* that Wayne spoke about soon. But the time is not yet.

It was still 1939. Reviewers were having convulsive reactions to the picture that revolutionized Westerns and John Wayne became America's great new hero on horseback. Even the supporting players had it made. Thomas Mitchell became one of the most sought-after character actors in Hollywood; Miss Trevor suddenly found herself in such great demand that even the Broadway stage beckoned and became part of her new environment; and John Carradine was catapulted into new and significant lead roles.

And Wayne?

He had been making pictures so fast and furiously that four oaters that had been filmed at Republic prior to *Stagecoach* and had been sitting in the can for timely releases, were disgorged in the nation's theaters. Republic was thus able to ride on the coattails of *Stagecoach*'s great success as Wayne galloped through *The Night Riders*, *Three Texas Steers*, *Wyoming Outlaw*, and *The New Frontier*.

With the thunder of *Stagecoach* still reverberating across the land, Duke sought a new frontier at RKO. Here he was teamed again with Miss Trevor, and with Brian Donlevy and George Sanders, in *Allegheny Uprising*, a stringy yarn about Indian warfare. Then he went back to Republic and, with Raoul Walsh directing, Wayne hooked up with Miss Trevor again and with Walter Pidgeon in *Dark Command*, another pretentious Western which was a surprisingly big success.

But right here the cycle of big Westerns, started by *Stagecoach* only the year before, started petering out. At this point, John Wayne seemed to be tottering on the edge of the cliff. Was he going to fall off the precipice and land in the saddle of ordinary sagebrushers again? Or would he go on to better things?

As he had once before, John Ford came to the rescue. He had bought a book based on some plays by Eugene O'Neill, and the leading character was a Swedish sailor. Marion Michael Morrison, of Winterset, Iowa, of Irish-Scottish parents, was picked for the lead.

"I can't do it," he protested to his old friend.

"Of course you can do it," Ford insisted.

The Long Voyage Home, an hour-and-a-half-long epic which teamed Wayne with Thomas Mitchell, Ian Hunter, and Barry Fitzgerald, was recognized as one of the few great pictures of 1940–41. Again Wayne's performance was nothing to rave about, yet he found himself in the middle of such noisy bidding that he felt like a bundle of tobacco.

Wayne made three other pictures in 1940, *Three Faces West* and *Melody Ranch* for Republic, and *Seven Sinners* for Universal. *Sinners* saw the Duke costarred with the most famous lady he ever had the distinction to play with, Marlene Dietrich.

No sooner was he through "sinning" with Miss Dietrich than John's Josie made her husband a father for the fourth time, on December 3, 1940. This time it was a seven-pound girl whom they named Melinda.

For those who kept records of such matters, the rhythmic production of Wayne offspring at precise two-year intervals was something to wonder about. But if you have any suspicion that Duke and Josie lived regimented lives and did things by the numbers, remove it from your thoughts.

More and more now Wayne was becoming independent of his wife. It's not clear whether Duke's enforced location-separations were the cause, or simply a possible sense of inferiority to the elegant Josephine. Whatever the reason, he seemed now to have acquired a new assertiveness in his manner which contributed even more to the differences between them.

Wayne was beginning to be seen with his friends more often. He went on hunting trips with Ward Bond and John Ford, he played more poker with them, and he seemed to be drinking harder, too.

But his movie work was never neglected, although now his pace was drastically altered. Instead of making a picture a month or more, as he had done the last dozen years, he reduced his workload to a bare minimum. In 1941, for example, he made only four films. That was still almost twice as many as the average big-name star was making.

His vehicles that year were *A Man Betrayed, The Lady from Louisiana,* and *Lady For a Night,* all for Republic, and *The Shepherd of the Hills* for Paramount which costarred him with the redoubtable Betty Field.

Not long after filming had finished on *Shepherd,* the Japanese bombed Pearl Harbor and America was plunged into World War II. Marion Michael Morrison had been too young to enlist during World War I and now, although not too old to fight for his country, John Duke Wayne was nevertheless beyond reach of the armed services. As the father of four children, he was draft-exempt, but as the star of several war films he would still make a major contribution to the defense effort.

Meanwhile, the stature Wayne had achieved as the Ringo Kid in *Stagecoach* and in his roles in subsequent films, especially with Marlene Dietrich in *Seven Sinners,* attracted the magnificent Cecil B. DeMille, who decided to team John Wayne with Ray Milland opposite two of the era's most glamorous actresses, Paulette Goddard and Susan Hayward. It was a typical DeMille extravaganza which cost Paramount $4 million. Its title: *Reap the Wild Wind.*

Paramount reaped plenty of profits from the film, too.

When an actor can go from a DeMille to a Frank Lloyd direction, he has really arrived. And that was Duke Wayne, who was reunited with his old "sinning" partner Marlene Dietrich in *The Spoilers,* directed by Lloyd for Universal.

In Old California followed and then came Wayne's first wartime contribution to the movie-going public, the action-packed drama *The Flying Tigers*, directed by David Miller for Republic. MGM then grabbed Wayne, teamed him with Joan Crawford, and threw them to director Jules Dassin, who one day in the distant future would be lionized for directing Melina Mercouri in *Never On Sunday*. Dassin was not lionized for this effort, called *Reunion In France*.

By the time Wayne finished his last film of 1942, *Pittsburgh*, which again hooked him up with Miss Dietrich, perpetuating rumors that Duke and the German beauty were "sinners" off-screen perhaps more than on, rumblings that might tend to confirm such an alliance were beginning to emanate from the Wayne household.

John and Josie were no longer able to make a go of their marriage. Michael was now eight years old; Toni was six; Patrick, four; and Melinda, two. But their parents were said to be at each other's throats. At least that was one of the stories. Another version, a much later one, indicated that John and Josie never had any arguments at all—until they ended their marriage in 1944.

That one was hard to believe.

There had been stories in newspapers and magazines about how John and Josie didn't see eye to eye about their religion and how Duke disliked the social whirl that Josie thrived on, but it is most probably nearer to the truth to say that John Wayne found himself another *Josie*.

It's an old Hollywood adage that when a man is successful he's never lonely. When John and Josie began to drift apart, he found new associations and new pleasures to react to. And these two factors were destined to bring an end to what had seemed to be one of the movie citadel's most ideal marriages.

It happened in Mexico City in early 1944. Duke Wayne had gone there with Ward Bond, Fred MacMurray, and Ray Milland in a joint effort to buy a local studio which they planned to set up as their own independent film company. They failed in that mission, but Wayne met the glamorous Mexican movie actress, Esperanza Bauer, who had starred with Arturo de Cordova in the south-of-the-border version of *The Count of Monte Cristo* and who had a remarkable first-glance resemblance to Josie.

But there all resemblances ended. Esperanza, who was thirty, was ten years younger than Josie. At the time, Duke was thirty-seven. Although Esperanza, like Josie, was tall, slender, and dark, the two women had nothing more in common. The complete antithesis of Josie, who was reserved and had a patrician appearance, Esperanza was hoydenish. When she smiled, her pug nose and the skin around her eyes, indeed her whole face, wrinkled. She had snapping black eyes and a smile that could charm the birds off the trees.

Yet it was her nose more than anything that fascinated Duke that night on the dance floor in Mexico City, prompting him to give her a Spanish nickname—Chata—which, freely translated, means "sweet little pugnose."

Oddly enough, she had been married in 1941 to a fellow named Morrison, Wayne's real name. This guy's first name was Eugene. She had divorced him the same year they were married.

But we are ahead of our story. It is still only 1943, a year when John Wayne would make but two movies, *A Lady Takes a Chance* and *In Old Oklahoma*. The next year was no different. He made only two films in 1944—*The Fighting Seabees* and *Tall in the Saddle*, a film in which his long-time pal Ward Bond costarred.

Toward the end of 1943 word leaked out to the newspapers that John and Josie had busted up, and John Ford called the Duke.

"I'm going on a cruise on my yacht," Ford said. "Come along."

When the Duke arrived, Ford said, "I'm worn out and I don't want to be bothered with conversation. So keep quiet."

Wayne kept quiet. Both men knew that neither was fooled by this lie. But, again, it showed the caliber of their friendship.

Duke supposedly never talked to Ford about his breakup with Josie, and if he wouldn't talk to Jack, he'd talk to no one else.

Shortly after his return from Mexico City, John Wayne went to New Guinea to bolster the morale of America's fighting men there, then returned home and made an agreement with Josie, who had learned all about his encounter with Chata in Mexico City.

They struck an agreement on these terms: Duke would forget about Chata if Josie never mentioned her name. Two minutes later, Josie brought up the subject again. From then on it was no go.

Even so, because Duke's love for his family was so much stronger than his desire for happiness just for himself, he stuck with Josephine—for a while. But the reconciliation failed to jell.

Though John Wayne had been married to Josephine Saenz more than ten years, the irony of it all was that he had never gotten to know much more about her than he had the day they were wed.

Divorce finally came for John and Josie. It was a dignified

finale in which the Big Duke agreed to give his wife, not only the custody of their four children, but their home, a fifth of his first $100,000 gross income each year, plus 10 percent of everything above that. In most years to come she would receive as her share of Wayne's earnings about $60,-000.

After four more pictures in 1945—*The Flame of the Barbary Coast, Back to Bataan, They Were Expendable,* and *Dakota*—John Wayne took almost a whole year off from film activities, his first cessation from movie-making in more than fifteen years.

On January 17, 1946, Duke Wayne married Esperanza Bauer at the United Presbyterian Church in Long Beach, California, with Ward Bond as best man and Mrs. Olie Carey, wife of the late Harry Carey, as matron of honor. The newlyweds' reception was held at the home of Mrs. Sidney Preen, also in Long Beach.

Why the home of Mrs. Preen?

Simply because Mrs. Preen happened to be the former Molly Morrison, Marion Michael's mother.

John Wayne and Esperanza Baur take out wedding license, January 16, 1946. They were married following day in Long Beach, California.

Wide World Photo

The Duke with his son Michael from first marriage to Josephine Saenz (1951).

American Airlines Photo

John kisses Esperanza goodbye before flying to London for premiere of *Rio Grande* (1951).

Wide World Photo

No more kisses for Duke and Chata, as Esperanza was nicknamed. They are shown ignoring each other during recess in divorce hearing (1953).

Wide World Photo.

Closeup studies show solemnity of couple during appearances on witness stand. Chata has asked $13,091.12 a month alimony and Duke tells the court she should be able to get along on $900 a month.

Wide World Photo.

Wayne complained about Chata's doodles because, as Duke told the judge, it meant Nicky Hilton was on Mrs. Wayne's mind. Divorce was granted.

Wide World Photo.

When son, Pat, now 16, starred in TV drama, *Rookie of the Year,* Wayne was delighted to play supporting role (1955).

Eastman Kodak Photo

Toni is a big girl now as she leaves church with bridegroom, Donald L. LaCava.

Wide World Photo

Duke and pretty Peruvian actress Pilar Palette, by this time happily married, change planes in New York enroute to Europe to do *Legend of the Lost* (1957).

Duke takes time out from filming of *The Alamo* to play daddy's role for Aissa, who is now three years old. He is telling her how nicely she did in her debut performance before cameras (1959).

Wide World Photo

While Wayne was in Japan making movie, his $250,000 home in Encino is gutted by fire. Pilar and baby Aissa, then 20 months old, escaped with servants (1958).

Wide World Photo

Duke and Pilar in New York for premiere of *The Alamo* (1960).
Metropolitan Photo Service

Now it's Melinda's turn to traipse to the altar and the lucky guy is Gregory Robert Munoz (1964).
Wide World Photo

No matter how many children come into his life, Duke's always the proudest papa. This is Marisa Carmela, born February 22, 1966, making her camera debut with daddy and mommy.
Wide World Photo

The Duke is caught in vise-like grip by a young tenderfoot on set of *El dorado*. He's John Ethan, three, another chip off the old block (1966).
Wide World Photo

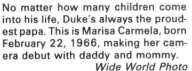

My, how Marisa has grown in two short years! And she's delighted to be with daddy on Hollywood set of *The Green Berets* (1968).
Wide World Photo

It's all in the family, you might say. Mustached Patrick is working with brother, Mike, in tradition of many Hollywood offspring who follow footsteps of their famous parents. Don't let the scowl fool you—Duke's thrilled (1971).

Wide World Photo

The Duke's gentle side is showing again. That's Michael Ian Wayne being embraced by the Big Guy during a break in shooting of *Big Jake*. Mike, who's three-and-a-half here, is Patrick's son, which makes John Wayne his granddaddy. It's tough keeping count on the Duke's geniological tree, but at this point in 1971 there were 18 grandchildren.

Wide World Photo

John Ethan, now nine, is protected from a band of kidnapers by his real-life father in this scene from *Big Jake* (1971).

Cinema Center Films Photo

CHAPTER VIII

Angel and the Badman

"When you have four children you love, contemplating a separation is a tragic and soul-searching experience," John Wayne said as he looked back on his divorce from Josie Saenz, "it's a real tragedy when you realize that a break is inevitable . . ."

Wayne pulled aside the curtain that had hidden some of the terms of the divorce for all those many years.

"I gave Josephine and the children everything we had accumulated together. I drove away with just one thing— a car. And since then I set up trust funds that took care of Josephine and provided for the education and protection of the children. Since that day, Josephine had the burden of bringing up the children, and I have always been eternally grateful to her for that."

Wayne recalled an episode that took place when Toni was eight. She had gone to a party. One of the women there expressed pity for her because she had no father at home.

"You poor child," she said. "You must have a wonderful mother."

Toni gave her a chilly look.

"My daddy's wonderful, too," she said.

"This couldn't have happened if Josephine hadn't been so fair with me in handling the children," Wayne observed. "I was able to remain part of their lives. I shared Josie's anxieties when they needed their tonsils out, worried about the braces for Melinda's teeth, or glasses for Toni."

Wayne would even take his big son, Mike, on hunting trips with him and on explorations in the desert. Later on, he'd go with Pat on fishing trips and they even scouted the coast of Catalina Island together.

And all this went on while Wayne was married to Chata —a marriage that didn't take Duke long to realize was "like shaking two volatile chemicals in a jar."

We will come back to those "chemicals in a jar" after they have had a chance to *mix* a bit and begin producing their explosive vaporescence.

John Wayne's long layoff from films after *Dakota* ended with his return to the RKO lot for his first fling into comedy since his disastrous and, as he termed it, "embarrassing" experience in drollery, that thing called *Girls Demand Excitement* back in 1931, which had helped earn him his walking papers at Paramount.

But RKO was not apprehensive about doing a John Wayne comedy at this particular point in time, 1946. It wasn't likely to be a dud because all the ingredients for success were present. Wayne, for one thing, was rapidly becoming one of Hollywood's top ten box-office attractions. His previous movie for RKO, *Tall in the Saddle*, was still making noise at the box office—and that was a picture nobody had wanted to produce.

Wayne had read the script of *Tall in the Saddle* in 1942 and had tried to convince everyone, including John Ford, that the picture was "perfect" for him. But only one man listened to Duke, Robert Fellows. He invested $700,000 in its production and even now, as Wayne was handed the script for *Without Reservations*, RKO already was counting a gross of $4 million on *Saddle*.

Wayne was really box-office. But would his fans come to see him in a comedy? RKO took out plenty of insurance just in case there was a revolt among his followers. The studio assigned the direction to Mervyn Le Roy, the master craftsman of bedroom comedy, and tossed in Claudette Colbert and Don Defore for good measure. *Without Reservations* went over smashingly.

After more than fifteen years as an actor, John Wayne had acquired certain habits he couldn't shake. One of these was that he never allowed himself to stay out of a cowboy or frontiersman's outfit for any length of time. Playing in Westerns had become second nature with Wayne—and a matter of principle. But most of all it made good $ense (dollars and cents) to him. Big Duke had taken his place besides the likes of Clark Gable, Gary Cooper, Cary Grant, and Humphrey Bogart by riding more horses and making more money than all the Kentucky Derby winners combined. Why should he forsake the saddle?

So it came to pass that Duke's next vehicle after *Without*

Reservations was *Angel and the Badmen*, which was made at Republic and which was notable only for the fact that Gail Russell was Duke's leading lady.

This may not seem too significant since Wayne by that time had played with more than any man's share of filmdom's most illustrious thespians—including Marlene Dietrich, Joan Crawford, Ella Raines, Paulette Goddard, Susan Hayward, Joan Blondell, and Betty Field, to mention only a few.

But as future events would indicate, Big Duke, the hero as always in *Angel and the Badmen*, might have been a bit of a *badman* himself with the *angel* of this epic—when they weren't in front of the cameras. It happened after director Edward Grant had given his last command on the set: "Cut! print it!"

It was time to celebrate and the members of the cast, so the story goes, headed for somewhere to revel over the picture's completion. The party lasted well into the night and into the wee hours of the next morning.

Back in their luxurious $125,000 hacienda in the San Fernando Valley, to which Duke had moved her after their marriage, Chata was chittering nervously with her mother (who was now living with the Waynes).

"Why hasn't he come home yet, why . . . why?" she was saying. It was 2:00 A.M.

Chata knew that there was going to be a party and she thought she knew where she might locate her husband. So she phoned Miss Russell's house. To her surprise, as she was to say later, the person she talked to on the other end referred her to a motel in the San Fernando Valley.

This infuriated Chata to such a boil that when her husband finally reached home at around four or five in the morning, she wouldn't open the door. It also happened that he didn't have his key.

"Aw, come on," she heard Big Duke saying, "let me in . . ." But Chata adamantly remained upstairs with Mama.

Soon the señoras heard the sound of breaking glass. They didn't know it but Wayne had put his fist through the glass panel and opened the door. To this day Chata swears that she wasn't aware it was her husband who'd broken in. She thought it was a burglar.

And that is why she charged downstairs in the dark gripping an automatic pistol which Wayne had taught Chata to use for protection. When she saw a form lying on one of the sofas, she pointed the gun at it. But Chata's mother prevented her from pulling the trigger.

"Stop!" she cried. "Eet ees your 'usband!"

Those volatile "chemicals in a jar" that Wayne spoke about were seething and about to explode.

Chata demanded to know where John had been.

He admitted that he'd been over at Gail's but swore that everything had been on the up and up. "Her mother invited me for a drink," he said.

But why wasn't he there when she called, Chata wanted to know? Big Duke had an explanation: When he left the studio with Miss Russell, they were following other members of the cast to a party but "lost them." So he and Gail stopped at several bars, then went to her house.

After a few drinks there, Duke explained to Chata, he hailed a cab and came home.

A cab? What happened to the car?

Well, that was another story. Gail, it seems, was working over at Paramount when director Edward Grant was beginning to cast for *Angel and the Badmen,* and somehow Wayne didn't think RKO had offered her enough compensation for coming over to slave in his picture. So he felt she had a little something extra coming to her.

Actually, Duke explained to Chata, it wasn't his car that he gave to Gail. Oh, no. He simply made the down payment on a new car for her. Not his car—just a *down payment*. "Fine theeng!" Chata screamed at Duke in her broken English. "You stay all night with that woman and then you geeve her a car!"

"No," Big Duke futilely tried to clear the air, "I just gave her the down payment . . ."

Nine months later, when he finished working with Laraine Day in another RKO non-Western called *Tycoon*, John Wayne headed straight home. There was no party to celebrate the finish of this film. But that didn't necessarily mean Duke and Chata were getting along. The truth of it was they weren't.

Until his marriage to Chata, Wayne had always been the big drinker in any house he lived in. Now he found he wasn't—his wife was trying to outdo him!

But John Wayne never carried his domestic problems to the studio and his work in films never seemed to suffer from his troubles with Chata. If anything, Duke's star was still in the ascendancy. By the end of 1947, it was going to shine brighter—John Ford was directing him again in another spectacular Western, *Fort Apache*.

The cast for this action-packed Indian War classic included Henry Fonda, Shirley Temple, and the man she'd soon marry, John Agar. When Wayne finished work in this film he went from the RKO lot to United Artists where Henry Hathaway directed him in *Red River*, then over to

Metro-Goldwyn-Mayer where the call again came from John Ford.

In all the years up to then and all the years since, Wayne never turned down Ford. Without question he has taken any part that the veteran director suggested. Wayne's implicit trust in Ford's judgment goes back to that day in 1928 when Jack launched Duke on his movie career.

"I owe him everything and there isn't anything I wouldn't do for him," Wayne has said a thousand or more times. "I know he'd never offer me any part that he didn't believe was right for me."

The film Ford called him for was *3 Godfathers* and the cast included another of Ford's and Wayne's cronies, Ward Bond. The leading lady was Mae Marsh, which leads us to Wayne's next leading lady and the next round in the battle of San Fernando.

When Chata heard that Gail Russell had been cast to play with Duke in *Wake of the Red Witch*, it was almost the livin' end. Her fiery temper made her fly into a rage. She packed and headed for Mexico City. Suddenly something seemed to happen to Wayne. He began to work hard again.

After finishing *Red Witch*—without reports about any more down payments on Miss Russell's cars—he made *The Fighting Kentuckian*. Then came *She Wore a Yellow Ribbon*, with Wayne receiving wide critical acclaim for his role as a Cavalry officer. In years to come, Wayne would claim that he had been nominated for an Academy Award for his part in *Ribbon*, but the records fail to show that. His first nomination for an Oscar would not come for another year.

Wayne made four films in 1949 instead of one or two. He didn't regret it when the results of the 1949 *Motion Picture Herald* survey came in.

Bing was no longer king. After five years as movie box-office ruler, Crosby had been deposed by the heir apparent, his companion in many a gag-strewn movie road and divot-pocked golf course—Bob Hope. Crosby wound up second in the poll, Abbott and Costello third.

And who was fourth?

John Wayne, of course, who had come up from nowhere. After a full generation as an actor, the Big Duke's fans had lifted him by the chaps and saddled him on movieland's most prestigious "horse" whose every clop kicks up gold dust. In Hollywood, where the art of acting has always taken a back seat to the art of making money, an actor's worth is measured in the final analysis by what he draws at the box office. If he doesn't draw, the attitude is: Who needs him?

No one was saying that John Wayne was a bad actor, or that he was a good one for that matter. But popular? Yes, indeed. And the Duke, although he couldn't know it yet, was heading toward even loftier heights of acclamation.

But fourth was fine for him now and it made him real proud, for look at who followed him on the list: Gary Cooper, Cary Grant, Betty Grable, Esther Williams, Humphrey Bogart, Clark Gable, James Stewart, Randolph Scott, Red Skelton, Clifton Webb, Loretta Young, June Allyson, Alan Ladd, Roy Rogers, Dan Dailey, Olivia De Havilland, Robert Mitchum, Claudette Colbert, Gregory Peck, Spencer Tracy, and Jane Wyman.

In a way, however, John Wayne's ascendancy was a puzzle to many Hollywood know-it-alls. For in 1948, when he was a lowly thirty-third in the *Motion Picture Herald*'s survey, he had banded together with a group of movie-capital biggies and formed the Motion Picture Alliance for the Preservation of American Ideals. Among those comprising the group were MGM production head Jim McGuinness, directors Leo McCarey and Sam Wood, Adolphe Menjou, Ward Bond, writers Borden Chase and Morris Ryskind, and Roy Brewer of the American Federation of Labor.

Their goal was to fight the inroads that the Kremlin was making in the film citadel. Or, as Wayne put it:

"An actor is part of a bigger world than Hollywood. That was why I plunged into the anti-Communist fight. I had never been a politically active person, but for a long time I had been conscious of the infiltration of Communists and fellow-travelers into the picture business."

The morning after the group, which met in McGuiness's house, had made its formation known to the press, Wayne received a call from a top studio executive.

"Duke," he said, "you've got to get out of that MPA. It will kill you at the box office. You will hit the skids . . ."

He certainly did hit the skids—from thirty-third in the ratings *up* to fourth. And the Big Duke still didn't know how high *up* was going to be.

It was perhaps a measure of the times that this kind of irrational thinking in Hollywood and elsewhere in the country gave bakers, doctors, lawyers, and masons the right to sound off about their politics, but denied it to actors, because they were not only more vulnerable to counterattack—but also more accessible to economic boycott, at the box office, by those who didn't agree with their philosophies.

Wayne did not back down after that call from the studio head. If anything, it made him display his patriotism with increasing enthusiasm as the months and years passed. And this feeling would ultimately reflect itself in many of his movies.

Despite all the doubts, including his own, about John Wayne's acting ability, the Academy of Motion Picture Arts and Sciences nominated him for an Academy Award as the best actor of 1950, thus taking a tremendous step toward dispelling those judgments of uncertainty.

But 1950 happened to be the year of Broderick Crawford's superb performance in *All the King's Men*—so, despite his memorable role as Sergeant Strycker in *Sands of Iwo Jima,* it turned out not to be Duke Wayne's year for an Oscar.

A few years later, when the Oscar was still eluding him, Wayne remarked:

"I always go to the Academy Award festivities each year in case one of my friends, who is out of town, wins an Oscar and I can accept in his behalf. I have received awards for Gary Cooper and John Ford. But no one—including me—ever has collected one for John Wayne. But that doesn't keep me tossing in my bed at night."

Then Wayne added wryly:

"Of course, it has happened that the fellows who own and operate theaters don't know that I am not much of an actor, and they have been foolish enough to pick me as the box-office champion of the year a couple of times . . ."

That honor as box-office champ came to Duke Wayne in 1950, the year after he finished fourth in the 1949 poll, and again in 1951. He won it twice in a row!

He wasn't such a *badman* after all.

CHAPTER IX

Exit Chata, Enter Pilar

Only Chata thought differently about John Wayne. To her, he was bad, bad, bad.

"All thee time he beat me up . . . he ees a terrible, terrible man," she was complaining. She was talking to an interviewer about the many fights and she was saying how she was going to leave the Big Duke, divorce him, and try to forget him.

Things between John and Chata had not been going well even after she returned from her Mexican vacation—without Mama, who had decided for health reasons to remain south of the border. It wasn't exactly that Senora Bauer was suffering from any particular ailment; it was just that she didn't want any more unhealthy encounters with the Big Duke.

Sometime in early 1952, when Wayne was on location in Honolulu filming *Big Jim McLain,* his rift with Chata finally was admitted to the public—by Chata.

The big bustup occurred while Chata was with Duke in the Hawaiian Islands. He had taken her along on a trip that he thought might help patch things up after their last bout at home. He considered it a "second honeymoon." But let's begin with that earlier fight.

It was November, 1951. For days, Wayne had been strolling around the huge house in Encino trying to make up his mind about his domestic situation. His wife and her mother were in the house, but he seldom saw them and never spoke with them.

Wayne also was thinking about the money situation. No actor was making more. He commanded $150,000 a picture now. But no actor was beset with more frustrating budgetary problems at home. Chata was spending as though money were going out of style. It was becoming like a treadmill for poor Duke. Late one evening, he came to a decision. He wrote a short note telling Chata that if she wanted him she knew where to find him. He packed a bag, caught a plane, and the next night he sat beneath the stars in Acapulco determined to sweat it out.

He sat beneath those same stars for nearly two months and nothing happened. As Christmas approached, he looked around and saw the Mexicans celebrating the season as only the Mexicans know how. The Yule spirit was everywhere except in the house Wayne had rented as a retreat.

Early the next morning, he flew to Mexico City and took the afternoon plane to Los Angeles. He did some shopping, then went home with an armful of gifts (he had even bought a present for his mother-in-law). But there was no reconciliation. The next night he was under the stars in Acapulco again.

By early spring, Wayne was tired of the separation. He wanted a showdown with Chata. He also had to keep the commitment to go to the Hawaiian Islands to film *Big Jim McLain*. He sent word through friends that he wanted to see Chata. By now Chata, too, wanted to see Duke. They got together in San Fernando and after a few hours of thrashing things out, Chata flew into John's arms. They kissed, agreed to end all this silliness and begin all over again.

"I've got to leave the day after tomorrow," Duke said. "But you come along. We'll go to the same places in the Islands we went years ago. Everything will be all right again. Wait and see."

They had a bridal suite on the boat, but they didn't need it after the first five hundred miles at sea. And shortly after they arrived in Honolulu, Chata Wayne took off alone and returned to mother and the house in the Valley. But only long enough to pack and head for Mexico City. After a few weeks, Chata returned—without Mama—and called her press conference to announce that she and the Big Duke were finished.

"Columnists have been printing cruel and untrue theengs about me," she complained. "Eet ees definitely true that I weel go ahead and take thee steps to get a divorce. I am terribly ill and deeply hurt and confused . . . more confused than anytheeng else. I have kept quiet for long time. As soon as I get feeling better and have chance to become oriented to thee crazy confusion that has taken place in thee last few months, I weel talk. And it weel be thee truth, thee entire truth that I weel tell.

"John ees the one who ees wrong. He ees thee cause of our marriage to be broken up. Thee first time we separate, I become very ill then, too. We patch that up, but we have more fights, many more . . . and now come thees. Thees ees definitely thee end of our marriage, Theengs cannot be mended anymore. Not after what happen in Honolulu . . ."

Wayne had gone off to Waikiki Beach to a party which, Chata claimed, featured some strip-teasers who really stripped. She said that John returned to her that night engraved with "a large black bite on the right side of his neck." Later, Wayne was to explain that he was bitten "against my will, without my consent, and without collusion."

But what really contributed most to the breakup was the memo pad the butler had handed to Wayne after he got back from Honolulu. The pages had some of Chata's doodlings. Duke studied the pad with inordinate curiosity, not to mention perplexity.

"Chata and Nick," said one doodle. "Mrs. Nick Hilton," said another doodle. "Esperanza Hilton," said a third doodle. There was no fourth doodle but three were enough for Wayne. His mind rushed back a half dozen years before. He was thinking about the times when he was courting Chata and the times after they were married. Chata used to doodle then, too. But her doodling then went something like, "Chata and John" and "Esperanza Wayne" and "Mrs. John Wayne."

"Nicky Hilton!" Wayne told himself. "What the hell's he been doin' here?"

He asked Esperanza. Her explanation: Nicky, who was no longer married to Elizabeth Taylor, had somehow injured his head. He was holed up in a hotel but Betsy von Furstenberg, the actress and German countess who was Nicky's cuddly bear at the time, wanted to take care of the nasty injury for him.

Since Chata and Betsy were friends, and since Betsy happened to be staying at the Waynes' as a house guest, what a wonderful idea if she could invite Nicky over and nurse his injury in the privacy of that great big twenty-room house. Betsy didn't think it would look nice if she were to take care of Nicky in the hotel room—even if his daddy, Conrad, did own that hotel and all those many others around the world.

Chata had no objection, so Nicky brought his head over to have it nursed by Betsy. The terrible thing about it all, as Chata was to say later, was that Big Duke—who wasn't home at the time—returned later and accused her of entertaining a man in his absence. She denied it. But Wayne was convinced, although he didn't know just who the man was.

Then he saw Chata's doodles.

"When I saw them," Wayne said, "I vomited."

You may begin to think that with all these troubles at home, John Wayne was too distracted to pay attention to the art of acting. Not so. Duke·was the busiest man in Hollywood and, indeed, he was also giving his children attention like the good father that he always was. In fact, when he went on location to film *Rio Grande*, he not only brought Michael and Patrick along, but he also let Mike make his acting debut in the picture.

Rio Grande was followed by one of John Wayne's few mistakes. He hooked up with that eccentric zillionaire named Howard Hughes to make a picture with an even more eccentric plot involving jet planes, spies, counterespionage, the whole works. It was called *Jet Pilot*. And this was one picture that John Wayne really put his heart into.

In the early stages of the film, a Navy pilot brought to the RKO lot as a technical adviser, gave Wayne instructions on how to "fly" a jet fighter. While in the cabin, the pilot said to Wayne: "And for Chris' sake have a little respect for that red handle there." He was referring to the ejector device which, when activated if a crash was inevitable, can hurl the pilot some seventy-five feet clear of the plane.

Late that night, after mulling over the idea and deciding it'd be great to have himself ejected in the picture, Wayne called the director, who was another eccentric, Joseph von Sternberg. Some twenty years before he had directed Gary Cooper and Marlene Dietrich in *Morocco.* Coop had reached a boil because Von Sternberg was directing Miss Dietrich throughout the entire production in German. One day finally, when he saw Coop yawn while he was talking to Miss Dietrich in their native tongue. Von Sternberg said angrily, "Iv you are schleepy you may go to ze home."

"Oh, no," Coop came back, "it's just that this is America and we don't understand this kraut talk."

Von Sternberg's accent had not improved greatly over those two decades—nor had his gruffness. When Wayne awakened him that night, Von Sternberg listened impatiently and then snapped this brief reply:

"Ven you are ze director you may eject yourself as often as you pleaze . . . ven I am ze director, I take orders from nobody . . . Now go schlaffen."

Next morning on the set, Von Sternberg approached Wayne.

"Duke," he said, "last night I had dream . . . vonderful

idea. I am putting crash scene in ze picture because I vant you to be ejected from ze plane . . ."

The picture had three stars: Wayne, Janet Leigh—and the planes that zoomed through the technicolor sky. And Hughes, who had made the wondrous discovery of Jane Russell and did wonders for her in *The Outlaw*, did likewise for Miss Leigh in this film by having her show her lines in all their stress and balance amid the flying aircraft.

When the picture was released, Miss Leigh was still a ripe twenty-two and there were no complaints about the way she busted out on the screen. Nor were there any squawks about Wayne, whose face has been one of the few constants in a shifting world.

But those jets! My, how they had aged! For reasons known only to himself, Hughes had not released the picture for seven long years after its completion. When it finally hit the screens in 1957, the 1950 jets, by aviation standards, looked like Tom Mix's Locomobile.

The picture, you could say, had aged in the can.

Wayne had no quarrel with Howard Hughes, however. Not when he was getting $150,000 a picture!

And with that kind of a salary, John didn't mind making even five pictures a year, as he did in 1951—*Reno's Silver Spurs Award, Operation Pacific, The Bullfighter and the Lady, Hollywood Awards,* and *Flying Leathernecks.*

The two *Awards* films were nine-minute shorts, but they only go to prove that Wayne was still following Will Rogers's credo.

It was after he returned from doing *Big Jim McLain* in the Hawaiian Islands that Wayne, fed up with the seemingly endless battles with Chata at home, decided to go on a safari or something to South America. His destination was

Peru. Indeed, he ended up in Tingo Maria, which is not a drink but a village that probably no one has heard of since the Incas.

There are a couple of versions of what happened. First we'll relate the former Pilar Palette's recollections of those events. Señorita Palette was Peru's leading actress and she was making a film on location in Tingo Maria when along came Duke Wayne, just visiting and probably trying to learn a trick or two from those clever Peruvian film directors. John had recently organized his own movie company with Robert Fellows. It was later dubbed Batjac productions, a name taken from *Wake of the Red Witch.*

"I recall that I was greatly impressed by his height, his width, and his strength," Pilar related about that meeting with the Duke. "When he shook my hand I felt as if I had been hit by a telephone pole . . ."

The picture that Señorita Palette was making was dubbed in Hollywood just before Thanksgiving of that year. And that's when she again saw the Duke, who had in the meantime gone to Ireland to film *The Quiet Man*, a departure from the usual Wayne Western and serviceman themes. The film was notable for other reasons as well.

Since his divorce from Josie, Duke had tried to see the children on weekends as often as he could. But because he was away on location so much of the time, there were long periods when he couldn't be with his kids. Josie would allow Duke to make up for these missed visits by letting the children stay with their father during the summer.

During the summer of 1952, Duke decided to give his two sons some responsibilities. He put Michael, now nineteen, to work in the office of Batjac, opening mail. Patrick, now fifteen, helped. Wayne wanted to give seventeen-year-old Toni a job but she was catching up on her studies in summer school. And Melinda, only thirteen, had to stay with Mom.

But during the summer of 1951 Wayne was about to leave for Ireland. That year, Mike had been working as a messenger at MGM, but when he heard about his dad's forthcoming trip to his ancestors' auld sod, he wanted to go along. "Fine," said the Duke. Then Toni heard about Mike going and got after Papa. Down the line it went. Before Wayne knew it, Pat and Melinda had counted themselves in.

In Ireland, Pat and Mike cornered the man who had discovered their dad. Pat, who had a tiny role in another of his father's pictures, said to John Ford:

"Uncle John, why don't you let us become actors in this picture?"

"Why not?" Ford laughed. "Everyone else is getting into the act."

Maureen O'Hara, who had the female lead, already had gotten two brothers into the picture, and Barry Fitzgerald also had a brother in it. Ford himself had cast a brother in a role and his son was assistant director.

Wayne had told his kids that he'd never stand in their way if they wanted to take up acting as a profession. But there was one condition that he would hold them to—they'd have to finish school first. Michael and Pat were undergraduates at Loyola University in Los Angeles and the girls were attending a Catholic parochial school in Pasadena.

The Quiet Man was a departure from the conventional Wayne movie, but it is best remembered for the bruising fight Duke wages with Victor McLaglen. He didn't want to fight, but Victor gave him no choice—poor, foolish Victor.

Ford was four days filming the fight, which was probably the longest knockdown drag-out fight in movie history. These tremendous sluggers fought all over the face of Ireland, knocking each other through closed doors, into rivers, and even battling up hills. Later, a friend viewing the film turned to tough-man McLaglen and gasped, "Jesus, Vic, you fellows really took a shellacking, didn't you?"

McLaglen chuckled. "John and I have been fighting too long to get hurt at this sort of thing."

On his return to Hollywood, Wayne quickly reported to the Warner Brothers studios to begin filming *Trouble Along the Way.*

It was while he was making this picture that Esperanza Bauer Wayne started making trouble by crying out: "Get me Geisler!"

This was a signal for famed Hollywood attorney Jerry Geisler to file Chata's divorce suit in Santa Monica Court. Not too surprisingly, Wayne's lawyer, Frank Belcher, also filed an action for divorce in Duke's behalf in Los Angeles Court—the very same day. But Geisler got to court at 11:50 A.M., fully forty minutes before Belcher. So it looked as though Chata's suit would get priority even if it was in another court.

To get back to Señorita Palette at the Warner Brothers lot where she was getting her film dubbed—and where, by the most incredible coincidence, *Trouble Along the Way* was being filmed. What do you think happened?

"We bumped into each other in the Green Room," Señorita Palette said.

"Hello, there," the Big Duke smiled as the Peruvian beauty choked on her ham sandwich. "I know you . . . Tingo Maria . . . Pilar?"

"It was," said Señorita Palette, "a sort of hands-across-the-Panama Canal goodwill invitation." For Wayne's next words to her were:

"How about having dinner with me tonight, Pilar?"

"I was lonely," Pilar explained. "I accepted. And I have had dinner with him almost every night since that day . . ."

Let's go back to Peru and to Tingo Maria a minute for instant replay of the scene of that first meeting between Señorita Palette and Senor Wayne. Only now this is from another angle—the camera is in the hands of Dick Weldy.

Dick Weldy was a big game hunter. He is a big, bruising, handsome man with leathery skin and blue eyes. Know anyone else who fits that description? Dick Weldy was also a fearless man. He didn't shoot lions, tigers, and deadly pythons—he caught them alive, then sold or rented them to circuses and movie companies.

Dick Weldy also worked as a kind of publicity executive for Panagra Airways and the reason he happened to be in the most unlikely locale of Tingo Maria that day was two-fold.

He was supposed to escort the distinguished Panagra passenger John Wayne around Lima and he was also supposed to find "some cuddlesome cuties as dates for the Duke." But, the story goes, "the babes in Peru just yawned off the chance to date big John." So Weldy, to save Wayne from boredom, took him to Tingo Maria to see first-hand how the Peruvians made their movies.

If Weldy knew then what he knows now, he'd never have taken Wayne on a "safari" to that last outpost—nor would he have dreamed of introducing Pilar Palette to John, as he says he did that day in Tingo Maria.

Pilar Palette, you see, was Mrs. Dick Weldy in private life.

"For the first few months we just enjoyed each other's company," Pilar related about what happened after that second meeting with Big Duke on the Warner lot. "It was not a big flashy burst of love. It came on gradually. We discovered we were miserable when we were away from each other. When I think back, I don't believe Duke ever really proposed to me. It was just understood that we would marry as soon as we legally could."

Well, in order for them to get married, we'll have to get them legally divorced.

Let's begin with Wayne . . .

CHAPTER X

A Mexican Standoff

Los Angeles Superior Court looked like the hippodrome as crowds battled to get into the arena where John and Esperanza Wayne were going to air their dirty linen.

So much had been written in the newspapers about the trial that spectators were already on the edge of their seats when Judge Allen W. Ashburn gaveled for order and Chata took the stand. Mincing no words, she quickly set the mood and atmosphere of the trial.

Questioned gently by her attorney, Chata told about the night that Duke spent at Gail Russell's house and the other time when he came back from the strip-tease party with that incriminating bite on his neck—and then she went into chapter and verse about the many times he had gotten boozed up and beat her.

118

"All the trouble I've had came out of a bottle," Chata said mournfully. Then she told about a series of parties at which, she claimed, Duke got drunk and beat the bejabbers out of her—before retiring and going to bed.

One such time was in 1946 in Honolulu, she testified. They were at the Moana Hotel when Duke came home from a nightclub party, grabbed her by one foot, pulled her from bed, and knocked her around the room a while.

Another time, in Mexico City's El Prado Hotel, he found her in the suite of another couple and dragged her by the hair down the hall to their suite, she said.

On another occasion, after talking things over with Herbert Yates, the president of Republic Pictures, Chata said, she advised her husband to accept a contract Yates was offering him. Wayne busted her in the nose for that good advice, she complained.

On still other memorable dates—in the San Fernando Valley, Honolulu, and other geographic hot spots—he walloped her, dowsed her with water, and hurled alcohol (rubbing, for Wayne was never known to waste the drinking kind) at her, she further charged.

And always, Chata went on, John's language was something awful. She was asked what he called her. She lowered her eyes in demure confusion. She was too embarrassed to repeat the words in the crowded courtroom.

"Whisper them to me," said Judge Ashburn.

The court stenographer, the lawyers, and the judge leaned close. She murmured the unmentionable words. Most of them were of the four-letter variety—and not one of them was *n-i-c-e*.

In short, what Chata was trying to tell the court, was that life with Wayne had hardly been anything else but six years of dodging fists and flying missiles. Then she floored the court and brought a smile to her husband's face.

"But he have heart of gold," Chata said. "I blame thee demon rum for hees behavior. After he sober up he always apologize."

Chata said there were very few times when Duke wasn't rambunctious. She recalled a night in Acapulco when he became enraged at her because she had blundered into a nude swimming party that he and some of his male friends were holding. She said that Duke had demanded to know what she was doing wandering on the beach and breaking in on him like that.

"Thees embarrass me terribly," she testified.

But the final straw, said Chata, was that night in Honolulu—she remembered clearly and distinctly that it was May 7, 1952—after coming back from a party.

"He take my shawl and throw it in the mud," Chata said. "When we reach our hotel room, he beat on the wall and curse me. Then I leave him . . ."

She had taken everything until then—from clouts with the back of Wayne's hand to whacks on the face from flying upholstered pillows. She was willing to kiss and make up after those assaults. But throwing her shawl in the mud—too much.

When she spoke about her encounter with her husband after he returned from his night-long date with Miss Russell and smashed his way into the house, Chata said:

"I tell Mr. Wayne I thought it very strange that he spend night with Gail Russell. He try to say that he could do that and that eet ees perfectly all right and I should not be upset."

Attorney Jerome B. Rosenthal, who was trying the case

in Jerry Geisler's place, made this observation for his client in court:

"This bewildered girl learned the horror of the bottle under the guidance, tutelage, and even under the roof of Mr. Wayne."

Then he revealed something that very few people knew—that Chata, while still Miss Bauer, came up from Mexico "to live for two years under the same roof with John Wayne while he was still married, though estranged, from his first wife . . ."

After that session in court, Wayne appeared upset over only one aspect of Chata's testimony—the introduction of Gail Russell's name into the fray.

"Why did she have to drag that poor kid's name into this?" Wayne said. "I never had anything to do with Miss Russell except to make a couple of movies with her. I deeply regret that Miss Russell's name has been brought up. Now I'm going to sling some mud myself . . ." He got his chance after the hassle over alimony payments was settled.

Meanwhile, when the judge reconvened court the next day, he announced that Chata would not have to testify further—because property settlement had finally been adjusted between her lawyers and Wayne's.

Strikingly dressed in a $200 Hattie Carnegie black taffeta suit, Chata smiled broadly. She had claimed that the Duke was earning at least $500,000 a year from his motion picture work and business investments, and she said that between the two of them they had been spending at least $13,000 a month. So, she asked for custody of their San Fernando home and $9,350 a month alimony.

In her itemized breakdown to the court, Chata showed the following monthly expenses:

For maintenance of the Waynes' five-acre estate, $1,245; household expenses, $1,983; automobile expenses (not including down payment on Miss Russell's car), $948; health and insurance, $1,518; support of her mother, $650.

You gotta believe it—John Wayne had been supporting Chata's mama and Chata had wanted Big Duke to keep on supporting her!

In a preliminary alimony hearing held prior to the trial, Superior Judge William R. McKay raised his eyebrows when he saw Chata's item for her mother. Wayne's lawyer told the judge he knew of no case where a court required a man to support his mother-in-law—after a divorce.

"I want to hear all about this," McKay said. "This mother-in-law situation frequently is the crux of a divorce contest."

Let's go on with the list:

Furs, jewelry, and personal effects, $499 (well, at least it was under $500); clothing, $746; gifts and entertainment, $261 (the Waynes didn't entertain much because they were feuding so often); charities, $1,023; travel fares, $794; telephones, $301 (mostly long-distance calls to Mama in Mexico City).

In his answer to the court, Wayne said that Chata was "extravagant" and suggested that she could get along on $900 a month, which he said he was willing to let her have. He even offered to pay another $1,300 for the upkeep of the estate.

Wayne further alleged that Chata had purposely kited the bills the past several months to make it look as though they had been spending that much, in order to support her claim for all the money she was demanding.

During this period of running up the bills, Chata evidently had done a better job than she anticipated. Just before the trial got under way, two county marshals came to her house and seized her Cadillac—because she had failed to pay liquor and grocery bills amounting to $2,367.

Judge Ashburn adjudicated Chata's claim by awarding her $1,100 a month for the next ten years—plus $10,000 attorney's fees and a $2,500 fund to handle auditing and investigation expenses that Chata's private eyes had worked up.

As for the house—Wayne got that.

As for Mama Bauer's support—the court said nix on that, too.

But Wayne wasn't through. He still wanted his day in court "to sling some mud" and the judge gave his side a week to prepare a response to Chata.

When Wayne finally took the stand, he put the shoe on the other foot, calling Chata the drunk of the family and saying that she was, in fact, nothing but a "disorderly bum." He denied that he had ever philandered or boxed her around as she charged.

Moreover, he firmly denied that he had romanced Gail Russell; as for that bite on his neck at the strip-tease party —well, this was his answer:

"It was a dull affair . . . It was my first stag party in six years. While I was sitting on a sofa this girl sneaked up behind me and bit me on the cheek—not the neck."

As Duke testified, Chata cupped her hands over her face and giggled. But later her expression became somber when she was called to the stand for cross-examination and admitted that Nicky Hilton had spent a week with her—when Duke was on location in Hawaii.

Wayne's lawyer, Frank Belcher, introduced into evidence

photostatic copies of those doodles of Chata's and Chata didn't seem to like that. Nor did she like it when John testified that he had never dragged her around by both feet as she charged.

"When she was well along in her cups at the Tony Lombardos'," Wayne said, "everyone else had left except Esperanza and her mother. So I took her elbows to get her to go home. She yanked herself away and fell on the floor. She threw an ashtray at me. It hit the wall and left a big mark. Then I grabbed her arm and leg and finally got her on her feet. I told her she was acting like a bum."

Wayne also told the court about the homecoming reception he had received on that Christmas Eve when he returned from Acapulco.

"I arrived home with an armload of presents to find that Esperanza and her mother had made up their minds that they were leaving me and going back to Mexico," he said. "I pleaded with Esperanza not to leave. She finally agreed to think over our situation—while in Mexico."

Chata's maid, Mrs. Agustina Roldan, took the stand and told the court that she was in the room once when Wayne struck his wife after expressing his disgust over an avocado sandwich.

Wayne went on to testify that he had never laid a hand on Chata—except in self-defense. He also testified about an episode at a nightclub when, he said, Chata was dancing with another man and fell on the floor.

"When I tried to pick her up," he continued, "she screamed at me that I knocked her down."

Hollywood scenario writer James Edward Grant, called by Wayne's side as a witness, testified that he had the impression from Chata that she had had an hour-long bruising fight with her mother in Mexico City.

"The next day," Grant said, "Chata told me, 'That son of a bitch hit me.' I laughed because I thought that was a funny appellation to hang on one's mother. But she told me she meant Duke, her husband, had hit her.

"I said, 'If that's so, it's the longest punch thrown in history because Duke was in Moab, Utah, making a picture.' "

Nicky Hilton, also subpoenaed as a witness, was never called to the stand. He was very put out.

"I'm the loser in this fight," he protested, referring to the box-office king's charge that he was the "other man" in the Waynes' stormy domestic life. Responding to the Big Duke's claim that Chata had doodled "Nicky" on the memo pad as if he were going to be her next husband, Hilton said:

"Everybody's left out the fact that I was a guest of Betsy von Furstenberg, not Mrs. Wayne. Betsy was my only reason for being in the house, not Chata."

There was nothing wrong with Nicky Hilton's head when he spoke in court.

In the end what really mattered was what Judge Ashburn had to say about the whole mess. His decision proved to one and all that he was a peace-lovin' man.

"I'm going to apply the humane principle of the California divorce law," Ashburn ruled. "I am granting a divorce to each party . . ."

That's what's known as a Mexican standoff. Neither party was held fully responsible.

Then the judge warned Duke and Chata that neither of them could marry for a year. If they did, he would charge them with bigamy!

The way John Wayne felt right then, he wasn't sure whether he'd ever want to marry again.

Yet six months later, when he was cornered by reporters,

he delivered a fifty-five-word speech that, for him, was the equivalent of a filibuster on the Senate floor:

"Pilar's brought me a great deal of happiness. I believe in companionship and I have to admit I like to be married. To the right girl, of course. But I'm not putting this wife on quite so high a pedestal. I like Latins. Some people like blondes, but I like Latins. I can't help it."

And you will see that, indeed, he couldn't help it . . .

CHAPTER XI

There's Nobody Like
the Duke

By the time he had gotten his divorce from Esperanza Bauer, John Wayne could look back on what was rapidly becoming one of Hollywood's most exciting careers. He'd been honing and buffing his man-of-the-West image for nearly a quarter-century and there were only a handful of actors who had either his longevity or his popularity on the screen. Only two other male stars were legitimately in the same unique class with Wayne—Gary Cooper and Clark Gable. Yet neither of them had appeared before the camera nearly as often as Duke. By now he had made 112 films and the end was nowhere in sight. Moreover, by this time he had achieved that most enviable of all niches in the Hollywood firmament—he was the No. 1 box-office attraction. And he had been that for two straight years.

What had brought John Wayne up to that pinnacle? Certainly his acting, his roles, and his films during the 1930s had done little to elevate him above the cut of routine second-class stardom. His performances as the outspoken, hairtrigger-tempered sagebrush hero who could straighten out his range enemies at every encounter and showdown contributed little to Duke's image on the silver screen. He had been a giant in physical stature but a dwarf so far as acting went.

By the end of the 1940s, Wayne had graduated to a totally new type of celluloid figure and the image seemed to reflect a man who was beginning to use more force and persuasion in his acting self. Duke had taken no lessons in dramatics since that ill-fated encounter in 1929 with the teacher who had tried to polish his voice and diction for his role in *The Big Trail*. Yet his experience in film after film gave him the basic equipment that no amount of teaching could provide. He had the hardware needed to handle the new roles of the 1940s which paved his way to the top.

Why had Wayne finally dethroned Bing Crosby in the 1950 box-office popularity poll of the *Motion Picture Herald* and become No. 1?

Everyone—actors, actresses, directors, producers, and fans—had a different explanation. Even Duke himself had his own view.

"It's not because I'm cheap, because I get a good pot of dough everytime I make a picture," Wayne mused. "I suppose my best attribute, if you want to call it that, is sincerity. I can sell sincerity because that's the way I am. I can't be insincere or phony. I can't say a petty thing and make it sound right. I'm just old honest blue eyes, I guess."

Another time, when asked to assess the ingredients that

had shaped his popularity, Wayne said, "Maybe people have seen me around so long they figure I'm one of the family."

By 1950, a whole generation of movie-goers had grown up with John Wayne and had watched his coming-of-age on the screen as though he were a vintage-year grape which had been squeezed and put into a cask to ferment with time into precious wine. That "cask" hadn't been really tapped until 1939 when John Ford took some of the juice, blended it into the first major production of the grape genus called Wayne, and labeled it *Stagecoach*.

Wayne's "fermentation" has continued, and there hasn't been a year since in which the vineyards of Hollywood have failed to produce a bumper crop of John Wayne movies.

If any further proof of the Big Duke's immense popularity were wanted, one only need consult the results of the 1951 *Motion Picture Herald*'s annual listing of money-making stars. John Wayne was again No. 1 on the draw; followed by Dean Martin and Jerry Lewis in No. 2; Betty Grable, 3; Abbott and Costello, 4; Crosby, 5; Hope, 6; Randolph Scott, 7; Gary Cooper, 8; Doris Day, 9, and Spencer Tracy, 10.

Time magazine was so impressed by the Big Duke's two-in-a-row top-place finishes that it did its first cover story on him that year and tried to put its finger on what made John Wayne tick and click.

"In 24 years of movie-making during which he has played some 150 imperceptible variations of the same role, Actor Wayne . . . has become almost a trademark of incorruptibility . . ."

Raoul Walsh, who gave Wayne his first starring role, offered another view:

"From the day I gave him a screen test I knew all he had to do was be himself. His personality, looks, and his natural mannerisms were made to order for motion pictures."

John Ford offered still another explanation:

"Duke is at the top for the same reason Gary Cooper, Clark Gable, and Jimmy Stewart have gotten up there—and stayed. He's a clean-cut, good-looking, virile, typically American type. Boys and men admire him. Women love him. They'd like him for a big brother, or a husband or a pal. Watch him on the screen. He's not something out of a book, governed by acting rules. He portrays John Wayne, a rugged American guy. He's not one of those method actors, like they send out here from drama school in New York. He's real."

Ford blew his stack when it was suggested that Wayne, along with Cooper, Gable, and Stewart were considered by some critics to be poor actors, below the so-called "artist class."

"All of them are great actors!" Ford snorted. "Wayne, Cooper, and Gable are what you call natural actors. They are the same off the screen as they are playing a part. Stewart isn't like that. He isn't a thing like he is on the screen. Stewart did a whale of a job of manufacturing a character the public went for. He studied acting."

Was John Wayne, at age forty-four, as uncomplex as that —a character who resolved problems the way the Ringo Kid did? Was he as much himself off-screen as on?

We know that John Wayne the man is a far more complicated animal. Josephine Saenz and Esperanza Bauer (and her mama, too) will attest to that fact. Yet despite the slop that was hurled in the courtroom during Duke's and Chata's divorce, Wayne emerged from the fray as he has done from every one of his movies—the embodiment of rugged virtue.

If the trial did anything, it enhanced his image to a world of film fans who until then had been wondering when Wayne would flaunt his sex appeal the way Gable and Cooper had done in their private lives with frequent head-line-making romances. Now his fans at least had gotten a glimpse into his off-screen 'life. And what they saw they liked.

Wayne couldn't be asked to become sexier on the screen because he wasn't like Gable or Cooper, both of whom could figuratively leap off the screen and seduce the maids and maidens in their orchestra seats. Big John did it more conservatively.

Oddly enough, Wayne has never concerned himself with projecting sex appeal on the screen. He admits that he never worries about his love scenes and doesn't try to be too adept. He thinks a little clumsiness is better suited to the characters he plays.

During the filming of *Jet Pilot*, Janet Leigh was ribbed about that on the set. "The guy wasn't very expert in the love interludes, was he?" she was asked.

"Maybe not," said Miss Leigh seriously, summing Duke up, "but he's very thorough."

As paradoxical as it may seem, it was in that very period of the early 1950s that John Wayne began to have deep sexual involvement with his leading ladies—on the screen. But always he played the lover's role discreetly, maturely, and without mushy sentimentality.

If ever there was a time in his life that John Wayne had grown to appreciate his own early maturity as a conservative man, it was during his encounter with Chata in Los

Angeles Superior Court. The battle of the alimony budget was not really fought by Wayne but by his old good friend and adviser, Bo Roos, who was responsible for Duke's present state of financial well-being.

Roos is a member of a fraternity peculiar to Hollywood and more recently to the world of professional sports—the business agent. Business agents take over the chore of handling the money of stars, for a 5 percent commission. They are not to be confused with agents who handle the stars' talents and get 10 percent for their services.

The business agent began playing a significant part in movie stars' lives when the wiser ones one saw how many other headliners had squandered their fabulous salaries. The business agent protects stars from all kinds of parasites who fasten on the money-makers—moochers, con men, thieves, and others who could spot a quick and easy way to siphon off the loot.

Wayne trusted Roos without reservation from the very beginning of their relationship, in 1940.

"I went with him when he showed me that an actor sometimes grosses as much as a small business, and even a small business can have its tax problems," Wayne explained. "Bo's clients come up fast and go down fast and it's up to him to figure out jobs that will best fit in with their security programs.

"That means he has to be rough with the studios, for example. They'd a lot rather deal with actors than other businessmen. It irritates them just to have Bo walk in. But he's in there pitching for his client and he's never afraid to make himself personally disliked if he can help his client."

Roos's first and primary step in handling a client is to make it clear that the money which comes from the client's work and investments goes to Roos. He puts his clients on weekly allowance—and he doles out the dough to them through a tight fist. For example, in 1952 he was giving John Wayne $40 a week walking-around money. Red Skelton, another of Roos's clients, was receiving $100 a week at the time—because he was walking around more than the Duke. Everything else the clients charged, and the bills went to Roos. And if they were spending too much he'd tell them.

"I had tried to keep Mrs. Wayne from being so extravagant," Roos explained about Chata. "But she never learned the meaning of the word economy. She wouldn't even try to stay within her budget. I even brought my wife in to talk to her but she laughed that off, too."

Though he failed to reform Chata, he never allowed her to dip into Wayne's capital—because Roos had safely invested it in diversified enterprises, including one such unlikely business as the Top Banana Company in New York.

A fair idea of Wayne's wide interests in those early days of the 1950s may be gleaned from Jerry Geisler's early alimony demands for Chata. The lawyer listed the names of 100 corporations and individuals with whom Wayne had business dealings and claimed that the Duke earned at least $500,000 a year through these sources.

Among those listed were such film studios as RKO, Republic, Warners, and United Artists. Celebrities on the list included Joan Crawford, Fred McMurray, Red Skelton, and John Ford. Geisler further claimed that Wayne also had $1 million in property.

Wayne's reply to these allegations was that he had only $500,000 in assets, and that outstanding obligations, including $150,000 owed for income taxes, made his net worth only about $160,000.

When Wayne was asked how much money he had earned just from films, he referred the question to Roos, who estimated that from the beginning Duke had probably made more than $15 million.

"We also tried to figure out how much his pictures earned for the producers," Roos added, "but we quit because the figures got so big they looked ridiculous, about as big as the cost of World War II."

"All I know," cracked Wayne, "is that I made a lot of people millionaires. Everybody but myself."

Even now Hollywood was beginning to feel the first faint inroads of that new medium called television. There was a demand for old pictures—any old ones. There were plenty of Wayne Westerns and they were taken down from the shelf, dusted off, and delivered to the video networks and independents.

As a result, John Wayne was suddenly "discovered" by the small fry and, though he was making nothing from the early films because he had worked in them for salary and not percentage, he still panned some of the nuggets in that new gold mine the studios were prospecting. He made money by endorsing a line of John Wayne cowboy suits and from such other varied windfalls as a John Wayne comic book series launched by Al Capp Enterprises.

But if you had listened to Jimmy Grant, the writer, tell it before he died, John Wayne sounded like the biggest Simple Simon since Roscoe "Fatty" Arbuckle.

"This big, lovable bum is one of the worst suckers you ever saw," said Grant. "He has blown over a million bucks on friends—or even some guys who tell him they went to school with him. It makes me want to shoot him.

"One guy came along and talked Duke into putting up thousands to raise a sunken vessel. It was supposed to be loaded with copper ingots. Duke never saw his money again.

"Then there was Tito Arias. A nice guy. Wayne went into partners with Tito on a business project—and Tito, he tries to start a revolution in Panama and loses Wayne's dough and his own dough as well."

Grant thought he had heard everything when Big Duke invested thousands of dollars with a motorcycle policeman who had stopped him for speeding.

"The cop had a big idea about manufacturing sugar sacks in South America," Grant recalled. "I was dumbfounded when the thing actually paid off."

Grant also rattled off the names of numerous movie people Wayne befriended to the tune of thousands of dollars.

"One was an alcoholic," Grant said. "He cost Wayne $70,000 in sanitarium treatment over a period of years, then committed suicide."

But before you begin to weep for Wayne, you may as well know that any money he squandered is a mere fraction of the loot he invested wisely and profitably. Even at that juncture of his career—1953—he was beginning to own all of, or part of, hotels, cotton plantations, oil wells, uranium mines, real estate subdivisions, and ice cream plants, as well as that factory which manufactured sugar sacks in South America. You name it—Wayne probably had invested in it.

John Wayne's reputation as a wizard of high finance far exceeds his notability as a fall guy. From the very beginning, Wayne was looking out for Wayne—not only financially, but professionally.

In 1947, he had had a clause written into one of his

contracts with Republic specifying that he could direct and produce a picture now and then. Part of the deal was that Wayne could have his own "executive" office at the studio.

A day came in late December, 1947, when the Big Duke almost lost the ceiling in his office, developed a first-class ulcer, and called his boss a jerk—all because of a dripping faucet that proved he couldn't call himself a real producer, yet.

In Hollywood, a producer is supposed to be a guy who gets things done. Up until then, however, Wayne had to admit he'd flunked in his efforts as a producer.

After Republic gave him his own office, Big Duke moved in and parked his six-foot-four frame behind the desk, his feet on top, and his head back on the chair. When Herb Yates, the studio head, walked in, Duke busily rustled papers on his desk. He was a great success as a non-producer until one morning he could hardly see his desk for the mist. He soon discovered what the trouble was.

Turning to his secretary, Wayne ordered, "Call a plumber to stop that damned leak upstairs."

"Yes, sir," she responded.

Minutes later the secretary came back.

"Mr. Wayne," she said, "I am informed by the accounting department that we will need a requisition from the maintenance department before the leak can be repaired."

Wayne eyed the flood that was building around his feet and ordered the secretary to draw up a memo to maintenance. Big Duke by now was trying to catch the dripping water in ashtrays and old film cans.

The maintenance department promised fast action. A week later, a man arrived. He looked at the ceiling.

"The leak," he told Wayne, "is not in your office."

"No," Big Duke replied, "it's *on* my office."

"Sorry," the man said, "I can't do anything about it because you don't have authority to authorize repairs outside your office."

"I'm not treated like this at other studios," Wayne protested, "and I'm supposed to be an executive here."

This was when *War Party* was being filmed by Republic. It was released under the title, *Fort Apache*, starring Wayne, Fonda, Temple, and Agar. The original title was kept when the film was released in England.

Wayne was furious at the many delays encountered in repairing that damn leak.

"Get the guy upstairs to sign the requisition," he snapped. "Here's a pen that writes under water."

In an hour the repairman returned.

"The office upstairs, sir, is vacant," he said.

The rain that had come into John Wayne's life continued to fall for the next two weeks. Meanwhile, Wayne swears, he got an ulcer from the aggravation. Finally, old man Yates walked in.

"Hmmmm," he mused. "You should get that ceiling fixed, John. Looks messy."

Yates grabbed the phone and barked, "Yates here. Fix the plumbing in Wayne's office.

In less than two minutes, three guys showed up with all kinds of wrenches. Five minutes later, the drip had stopped.

"That's better," Yates told Wayne. "If you want anything, let me know."

Wayne leaned over his desk in a boil.

"All I want to know," he snarled, "is who the guy is who started requisitions?"

"I did," Yates replied. "It works very well."

"Oh," Wayne almost cringed.

It wasn't too long before Big Duke had the requisition system working efficiently for him. A day came when he needed a new typewriter for his secretary. He picked up the phone.

"Yates here," he said. "I want . . ."

By the time he put down the receiver, two maintenance men were standing in front of him.

"Where do you want this placed?" the man holding the new typewriter wanted to know.

John Wayne had learned well about how a producer worked . . .

Duke's chance to produce didn't come until 1949. The picture was *She Wore a Yellow Ribbon*. Then came *Big Jim McLain*. Others would soon follow.

Big Jim, in fact, was bankrolled by Wayne-Fellows Productions, which Duke had organized with Robert Fellows, who had faith enough in John back in 1942 to invest that $700,000 in *Tall in the Saddle*, which Wayne had wanted to do. You may recall that the picture grossed more than $4 million. Wayne-Fellows was the first of Hollywood's so-called *independents*, but they still had to rely on the big studios to get their films maximum theater exposure in the country. Wayne-Fellows made such arrangements for distribution with Warner Brothers.

Even preparations for the divorce trial couldn't keep Wayne from acting in pictures. He made *Island in the Sky* during that period, which he coproduced with Fellows and then—after getting his freedom from Chata—headed back for his horse.

Wayne-Fellows, which subsequently underwent a change

of name to Batjac Productions, bought the script of *Hondo*

Wayne had negotiated with Glenn Ford to star in the picture but the actor didn't want to work with John Ford, no relation, and so John Wayne saddled up for the lead role. The picture grossed $4,100,000 which was a better than 500 percent return on Batjac's investment.

On Batjac's next film, *The High and the Mighty*, Spencer Tracy was proffered the lead role. When he turned it down, Duke took on the part of Dan Roman, the elderly copilot of an airliner that encounters engine trouble over the Pacific. Wayne's portrayal of the commander behind the controls of the plane, remaining calm and alert while everyone around him is going to pieces, was given high tribute by critics across the country.

This, together with *Hondo*, comprised the only two John Wayne films released in 1954, a year that followed two successive seasons in third place on the box-office polls. But by the last days of December when the *Motion Picture Herald*'s survey was again made known—John Wayne was back at the top, dethroning Gary Cooper, No. 1 in 1953. Wayne's "comeback" was credited to his superb performance in *The High and the Mighty*.

There was a third picture that Wayne had finished that year but it was still being edited. This was *The Sea Chase*, which was filmed off the Hawaiian Islands. Shooting was finished in the last days of October and then something happened. But before we get to that, let's go back two months to a scene in California.

John Wayne is escorting Pilar Palette up the steps of a white frame and fieldstone house set in the midst of the lush, rolling terrain of the San Fernando Valley, not far from the Clark Gable ranch. With its stately trees and green slopes, the house that Duke had once occupied with Chata looked more like a Kentucky farm than a California ranch.

The house had reverted to him in the divorce proceedings, as you may recall, and Big Duke wanted Pilar to have a look at it.

"I bought it in 1950," he told her. "I've hardly lived in it at all. But if you don't think you could be happy here, Pilar, I'll sell it and buy a home wherever you like . . ."

"I could be very happy here with you," Pilar told Duke.

"That," said Pilar later, "was the nearest I came to receiving a proposal."

When Duke headed for the beautiful Kona Coast of the island of Hawaii, he took Lana Turner with him—also David Farrar, Lyle Bettger, Tab Hunter, and James Arness. For they were all going to play key roles in *The Sea Chase*

But he also took Pilar Palette along. She had no role in the film—but would soon have one in his life.

It happened on November 1, 1954, against a flaming Hawaiian sunset and amid exotic tropical flowers . . .

The Duke in 1937.

In Three Faces West (1940).

The stalwart hero of *In Old California* (1942).

Wayne wears whiskers in *Back to Bataan* (1945).

A rugged moment in *The Alamo* (1960).

As General Sherman
in *How The West Was Won* (1964).

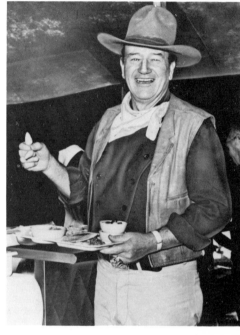

Time for chow in Durango, Mexico, during filming of *The Sons of Katie Elder*, the Duke's first movie after operation for chest cancer (1965).

This is what it's like for a junior officer staring into Duke's face. The steel-eyed squint of the gruff cavalry officer in *Rio Lobo* (1970).

UPI Photo

This is John Wayne's proudest moment as he takes a good, hard look at his first Oscar for his role as the one-eyed sheriff in *True Grit* (1970).
Wide World Photo

Claire Trevor is the Duke's valentine in *Stagecoach* (1939).

Martha Scott finds romance way out *In Old Oklahoma* with Our Cowboy (1940).

Young Matt is shepherding Betty Field with his trusty rifle in *The Shepherd of the Hills* (1941).

Marlene Dietrich seems to be enjoying this moment in *The Spoilers* (1942).

The Duke is having a stormy session with Ella Raines as he tries to show her who is *Tall In The Saddle* (1944).

A tender moment with Donna Reed in *They Were Expendable* (1945).

You shouldn't have any trouble figuring who is who in this scene with Gail Russell in *The Angel And The Badman* (1946). Gail also played a brief co-starring role in Wayne's real life, which you'll read about in this book.

Lana Turner and Big Duke are thrown together for days on end on the uninhabited South Sea island of Pom Pom Galli—and this is how it winds up. They made their waves in Sea Chase (1955).

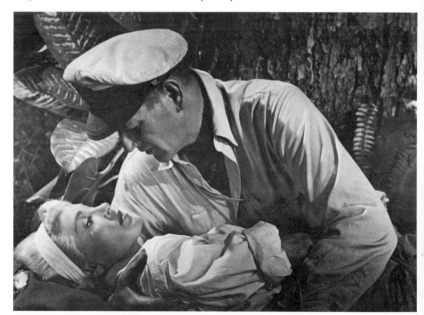

One nice thing about making a movie with La Turner. When all the shooting is done, there's that drudgery called posing for publicity stills. See how John Wayne scorns such work?

Ray Milland has his eyes on Paulette Goddard who has her eyes on John Wayne who has his eyes on a guy he's measuring for a right cross in scene from *Reap The Wild Wind* (1942).

CHAPTER XII

The Man and
His Principles

"Hello, Duke," the voice on the phone from Los Angeles said. "This is Frank . . ."

The call was from John Wayne's attorney, Frank Belcher. The news he had for Big Duke was that Judge Allen Ashburn had finalized Wayne's divorce from Chata—and the big guy was free to marry again.

John wasted little time going from the unhitching post to Pilar.

Pilar, too, was free to marry again, for her union to Richard Weldy had been annulled just a few days previously.

And it can be said Pilar wasted little time in going from Dick to Duke.

It happened that evening in the exquisite gardens of Territorial Senator William H. Hill's magnificent mansion, which he had loaned to members of the *Sea Chase* cast. The home once belonged to King Kamehameha III.

No one remembers the wedding more vividly than Pilar, who was a broth of a girl of twenty-four then—exactly twenty-three years younger than the Big Duke. In fact, Pilar had just turned twenty-four and that was an occasion she won't forget either because it happened a few days before the wedding.

"I almost murdered him," Pilar laughed. "All day long he said nothing about my birthday. I assumed he had forgotten it, and I was quite miffed. I went to my room early, took my make-up off, and was getting into bed when New Year's Eve broke loose.

"Everybody in the company, from stars to prop men, banged on my door. An orchestra played "Happy Birthday" and there was champagne, cake, and presents. And I looked like a ghost."

But on November 1, 1954, her wedding day, Pilar looked like Lupe Velez and Dolores Del Rio all wrapped up in one. She wore a pink organdy cocktail dress and, well, let her tell it . . .

"The house clings to a high promontory overlooking the bay," she said. "I'm positive it is the most romantic place in the entire world.

"The Hawaiians in Kailua closed up their shops, put on their best clothes, and came to our wedding. We were married on the senator's lawn by an Hawaiian justice of the peace just as the sun sank into the Pacific. I never hope to see such a fabulous sunset again."

The bride was given away by John Farrow, Mia's father, who was directing *The Sea Chase*. Wealthy California sportsman, Francis H. I. Brown, of Pebble Beach, acted as Duke's best man.

"After the ceremony, some 150 natives lined up with the cast and crew to kiss the bride," Pilar recalls. "I was well bussed. Then, as night came on, they lighted torches and sang and danced until it was time to leave for the airport. Here we were given a royal Aloha with all the trimmings . . ."

There was only one minor ripple on the otherwise placid waters upon which Duke and Pilar set sail as partners in life. During the filming, reports had filtered out of *Sea Chase* locations that Wayne and Miss Turner were feuding, and it was then said that she had hightailed it back to the States when the filming ended on the eve of the wedding, while the rest of the cast and crew remained behind to toast the bride and groom.

After the wedding the newly-marrieds flew to Honolulu and retired to the bridal suite of the Royal Hawaiian Hotel. Next day, they came out to greet reporters.

"This is the greatest thing that ever happened to me," trilled Wayne as he kissed his bride. "I've had lots of wonderful things happen but this is the best."

Most people, as Pilar put it, get married at home and fly to Hawaii for an island honeymoon.

"Duke and I reversed things," she said. "We flew home to California for our honeymoon."

That certainly was a reversal. When Duke married Chata at home, they went to the Hawaiian Islands for their honeymoon.

After Wayne and Pilar returned home, reporters cornered the lumbering actor and asked him whether he had a special preference for Latin gals, for Pilar was his third wife from south of the Border.

"It's just coincidence," Wayne smiled, ignoring his

previous statement about feeling a little something more for Latins.

"I've never been conscious of going for any particular type," Wayne explained now. "They say a man follows a pattern, but I haven't been aware of it myself. Each of the women I married has been entirely different.

"I certainly don't have anything against American women. As a matter of fact, my wives have been as much American as they have been Latin. None of them speaks with an accent [Maybe John, he forget, that Chata speak like *thees*].

"My first wife had a French and Spanish mother and father but she was brought up in Texas. Esperanza spent a lot of time in this country, not here, but in Florida and elsewhere. And Pilar has been here a great deal and speaks English perfectly."

Someone asked Wayne if Pilar would pursue her acting career.

"No," he replied emphatically. "She never had much of a career [which doesn't speak highly of those Incas we interviewed in Tingo Maria who told us Pilar was their country's leading actress]. Once Sol Lesser sent a crew to Peru to make a picture about hunting Inca gold, and they needed a girl to walk in front of the camera with bare feet and long hair. Pilar did it.

"Then an independent producer went down there to make a picture, using amateur actors, and she was in it. But I don't think the picture was ever released here."

Where would he and Pilar honeymoon, Duke was asked?

"At home," he replied. "We've been traveling all over the world and we'll be happy just to sit by the hearth for a while."

A reporter asked Wayne what his next picture would be.

"We're going to produce *Blood Alley*," he replied. "I've got Robert Mitchum and Lauren Bacall all set for the top roles . . ."

That was what he thought. Like Glenn Ford in the deal for *Hondo*, and Spencer Tracy for *The High and the Mighty*, Bob Mitchum couldn't work things out with Batjac—and Wayne ended up playing the lead again. His role in this film is that of an American mariner, thrust into an island jail by the Reds, who pilots the entire population of an uprooted Chinese village through the Formosa Straits to Hong Kong and consequent freedom from the Communist yoke.

More and more John Wayne was trying to work up an American sweat over Communism. His next production following *Blood Alley* was *The Conqueror*, directed and produced by Dick Powell and starring Susan Hayward, Pedro Armendariz, and Agnes Moorehead. The picture hardly had an anti-Red line in it—all it did was detail the early career of the twelfth-century Mongol leader, Genghis Khan.

Yet when released in early 1956, the film couldn't penetrate the Iron Curtain. The Soviet Union, which had indicated a desire to screen the picture in Moscow, decided at the last minute to ban this film about love and warfare among the Mongols and Tartars.

Wayne had hoped for a world premiere in Moscow and, in fact, he and Gary Cooper had made plans to fly to the Russian capital for that occasion. But the crew in the Soviet Embassy in Washington, who had been given a private screening of *The Conqueror*, said "*nyet.*"

That wily Nikita Khrushchev wasn't going to let John Wayne leave his imprint on American-Soviet cultural relations. John had already come out with too much clout against Communism—not only in films but off-screen. He was an *enemy* of Moscow.

Wayne's first awareness of the Communist threat against his country came in 1945 when he was making *Back to Bataan*. The director of the picture was Edward Dmytrk and Wayne says:

"He was the only guy who ever fooled me. But when he started talking about the masses—which is from their book, not ours—I knew he was a Commie." Dmytrk later admitted that he was a Communist during 1944 and 1945 before undergoing "a complete change of heart." Wayne said he was invited to a number of "cell" meetings.

"I played the lamb to listen to 'em for a while," he says. After that he washed his hands of Dmytrk and decided he'd do everything he could to fight Communism.

When Senator Joseph McCarthy and his House Un-American Activities Committee began uncovering leftists, John Wayne quickly rallied to his support.

Remember what Wayne had said about an actor being part of a "bigger world than Hollywood?" That was what precipitated his plunge into the formation of the Motion Picture Alliance for the Preservation of American Ideals.

Wayne saw himself as a patriot, yet next to some of his flag-waving colleagues he looked a little pink.

"We had a split in the group," scenarist Borden Chase reported. "The once-a-Communist-always-a-Communist group and the group that thought it was ridiculous to destroy some of those who, say, joined the party in the 1930s in Nazi Germany. Duke and I were in the latter group."

That's the reason arch-conservatives didn't regard Wayne wholly and purely as one of them—at the time.

Duke was willing to forgive and forget, and he tried to express these sentiments for Larry Parks, who had admitted his Old Left indiscretions. But Duke's praise of Parks only drew fire. Hedda Hopper scolded him publicly and reminded him of the boys who were dying in Korea.

Today, as in all the years since, Wayne has no stomach for Communists, past or present, repenting or unrepenting.

"I think those blacklisted people should have been sent over to Russia," he says. "They're yella bastards. They'd have been taken care of over there, and if the Commies ever won over here, why hell, those guys would be the first ones they'd take care of—after me." Then he added:

"My main object in making a motion picture is entertainment. But if at the same time I can strike a blow for liberty, then I'll stick one in."

Wayne's philosophy about an actor having to be part of a bigger world than Hollywood extended beyond political ideology alone. He viewed his own position as one which could further the fight against Communism in the center of the political ring . . .

During the last days of the 1940s and the early 1950s when he was grinding out some of his better horse epics, Wayne received unsolicited praise from a most unexpected corner—General of the Army Douglas MacArthur.

"Young man," MacArthur told Wayne, "you represent the cavalry officer better than any man who wears a uniform."

In 1952 MacArthur went to the Republican National Convention in Chicago where a group of his followers were beating the drums to nominate him for the Presidency. Wayne decided to attend the convention with other Hollywood stars who felt the nation needed their participation in politics.

Wayne's candidate was really Senator Joseph McCarthy of Wisconsin, the Communist-fighter. Another politician in greasepaint that year was famed actress Ruth Chatterton, who was stumping for a Democrat named Adlai E. Stevenson. Other Hollywood luminaries had other preferences. It was the film capital's first serious plunge into the political arena.

At the convention MacArthur received 10 votes on the first ballot, Governor Harold Stassen, 20; Governor Earl Warren, 81; Senator Robert A. Taft, 500, and another general named Dwight D. Eisenhower, 595. Ike was still 9 votes short of the 604 needed to nominate. McCarthy didn't even get a first vote.

No second ballot was needed. Minnesota dumped its favorite son, Stassen, and orders were given to print the "We Like Ike" buttons. John Wayne wore one of those buttons all during the campaign which saw Eisenhower win in a landslide over Adlai Stevenson that November of 1952. And Richard Milhous Nixon became Vice President.

Wayne never strayed far from the arena of politics after this. In 1956, he again associated himself with the movie colony's campaign to reelect the Eisenhower-Nixon ticket, but he didn't spend much time on politics that year. He was home much of the time listening to the pitter-patter of little feet . . .

"The nicest thing that has happened to us since we married is little Aissa Maria," Pilar Wayne said at the time. Aissa was born March 31, 1956, and she was, as Pilar put it, "a spitting image of her father."

"What a session her arrival was!" Pilar recalls.

"I awakened Duke in the middle of the night and told him we'd better get started for the hospital. 'Now don't get nervous,' he kept saying over and over while he dressed.

"I wasn't nervous at all. But I have never seen a man go so completely to pieces as he did. All the way to the hospital he kept singing, in an off-key, too, songs that he and his buddies, John Ford and Ward Bond, used to sing around the campfires in Utah. They were supposed to calm me, I guess. But they were not exactly songs to soothe an expectant mother . . ."

Big Duke should have sung a couple of the Bradbury numbers from his "orsy-opry" singing-cowboy days. They used to put audiences to sleep, so why not Pilar?

Wayne also should have taken Pilar to St. Joseph's Hospital on a familiar horse instead of in the car.

"He took a left turn when he should have taken a right one," Pilar went on. "He was thoroughly humiliated because he had lived in the Valley for half his life. Fortunately, Aissa was eleven hours late."

When Duke was admitted to the room to see Pilar and his new seven-pound six-ounce daughter, his wife thought "he would say something tenderly beautiful" which she'd remember for years.

"Move over," Big Duke grumbled, "I'm pooped." And he plopped onto the bed.

In the weeks and months that followed, Wayne would rush home from the studio, or his Hollywood office, every day to play with Aissa before her mother tucked her into her crib. When Aissa began to stand and talk, she'd say, "Daddoo," and do a cha-cha-cha for Duke, which always sent him into howls of laughter.

"It was wonderful to hear him talking baby talk to her,"

Pilar said. But she frowned on her husband's habit of constantly bringing Aissa large stuffed dogs and teddy bears.

"You are spoiling her something terrible," Pilar would say to her husband.

"I can spoil the baby," Duke would snort. "But you can't. Sorry, you'll have to be the villain."

For John Wayne, 1956 was also a very big year in another way. He had the pleasure of announcing to the press that he had become the highest-salaried movie star in the world. From then on he would get $666,666.66 per picture.

Wayne revealed that he had signed a contract with 20th Century-Fox, which was giving him $2 million for three pictures in the next three years. Figuring an average of eight weeks of shooting per picture, Wayne's gross paycheck would average out to almost $100,000 *per week*—more than most stars were getting for an entire movie.

Duke also let it be known that the salary was going to be paid over a ten-year period at $200,000 a year.

"Hey, Duke," a reporter said, "that means after you make the three pictures you can retire for life . . ."

Wayne, who was forty-nine now, smiled and answered, "Yeah, but I won't. I wanna keep workin'."

And he kept workin' and workin' through *The Searchers*, *I Married a Woman*, and *Wings of the Eagles*. Then came time to make another film under Batjac's banner, but the corporate structure had changed a bit. Wayne's partnership with Robert Fellows had broken up in December, 1955, after they had made a total of ten films.

Now Wayne reactivated his independent company, under the Batjac label again, and entered into a four-picture producing-distribution arrangement with United Artists. That was in addition to his three-picture $2 million deal with 20th Century-Fox.

The first project under the Batjac-UA setup was *The Legend of Timbuctoo* which was filmed in early 1957 in Italy, Tripoli, and Libya and costarred Sophia Loren and Rossano Brazzi. The picture never carried that title, however. It was renamed *Legend of the Lost.*

While Wayne was on location in Gadames, an oasis in the Sahara Desert, he cabled Pilar:

"It is beautiful here. Miss you. Please join me right away."

Pilar left Aissa with her mother (who like all the other mothers-in-law was also staying with the Waynes) and flew to her husband's side. Enroute, she changed planes in New York City.

You could always count on the late Dorothy Kilgallen to get the "inside" of every story. And she didn't miss "scooping" the rest of the town while Pilar was there switching to her trans-Atlantic flight.

"Mrs. John Wayne boarded a TWA plane for Rome yesterday afternoon for the most American reason in the world," wrote Miss Kilgallen. "Her husband, currently shooting a picture in Africa, cabled her that he wanted some hot dogs—desperately. So the dutiful Mrs. W. hopped from Hollywood to New York, the colorful Roosevelt Zanders met her with four large cans of frankfurters, and off she went to the Eternal City, where she was to take a plane for Tripoli and a final change to a jungle plane that will fly her (and the hot dogs) to her true love. (Do hope she remembered the mustard!)"

We put it down as a pretty good marriage—because Pilar *had* remembered the mustard.

Pilar, who had also worked as a Panagra Airlines stewardess for a brief time, had never gotten used to flying. This was a trip she'd not soon forget—it took four days to get to Gadames, which had only one building—a fourteen-room house which once served as a retreat for Italian General Italo Balbo, who led a squadron of planes across the Atlantic to the United States on a goodwill mission in the early 1930s—and then got his rump handed to him when Mussolini sent him to Libya as governor general. Mussolini thought Balbo was becoming too ambitious—and in June, 1940, the general was brought down while flying over Libya. By Italian gunfire!

Balbo wasn't much of a housekeeper either, according to Pilar.

"He had neglected to install plumbing," she said. "But, thank heaven, the movie company attended to that."

Balbo had also forgotten to install a hot plate—so they had to eat the frankfurters cold. Well, at least Pilar hadn't forgotten the mustard—so it was a pretty good marriage, after all.

The location was one of the roughest spots Pilar would ever visit with her husband.

"There were no phones or electricity," she continued. "As soon as the sun went down there was nothing to do but go to bed. We were up at five every morning to go to the location, and it must have been twenty below zero."

Duke had a room and a bath in the house. The rest of the cast, including Sophia Loren, also roosted in the house.

"One day," Pilar recalled, "Sophia had to take a bath in a stream that was supposed, for story purposes, to be hot and steamy. It was ice cold. Four times she took a bath in that icy water and never a whimper out of her, even when her lips turned blue."

Sometime after she returned with Duke to California, Pilar was asked by an interviewer if she was jealous of Duke's glamorous leading ladies.

"The answer is a great big no," she replied. "Unlike most wives, I am usually on the set when he does his torrid love scenes. If he does a scene well I say, 'That's just great, Duke.' I suppose it's because I was once a professional actress myself."

John Wayne went into a second production under the new Batjac corporate organization with United Artists after his return from Libya. The film was *China Doll*. Then he was off for Tokyo to keep the first of his three commitments for 20th Century-Fox, a film that had been given the tentative title of *The Townsend Harris Story*.

Wayne, playing the role of Townsend Harris, first American envoy to Japan (1856), was teamed with Eiko Ando for the portrayal of an essentially exotic yet tragic romance in the tradition of *Madam Butterfly*. But when the picture was finally released in this country as *The Barbarian and the Geisha*, John Wayne couldn't fool his fans. He was essentially the Big Duke under that kimono.

Pilar, who was to have gone along with her husband to Tokyo, remained at home for reasons not given. At least not at the time . . .

CHAPTER XIII

Pilar of Fire

It wasn't usual for Blackie to bark in the middle of the night. How many times the dachshund barked, Pilar can't say. But she finally heard him when she awakened sometime around three o'clock on that morning of January 14, 1958.

Pilar opened her eyes and saw a flickering light. Blinking, she looked around for the source of the strange light, saw it, and became terrified.

"Flames were licking at the edge of the carpet," she recalled.

Only a few feet away was the baby's crib. She could barely see it because of the smoke.

Pilar leaped out of bed, rushed to the crib, grabbed the sleeping twenty-two-month-old Aissa in her arms, and raced downstairs to an alcove. Aided by the dog's barking,

Pilar managed to awaken the two maids, Consuelo Saldana, and her sister, Angelica, and the child of one of the women.

"Call the fire department!" she shouted. Consuelo ran to the phone.

"Take the baby," she said to Angelica, handing her Aissa.

Pilar scurried back upstairs, a fire extinguisher in hand. She tried to put out the flames but . . .

"All of a sudden—woosh," Pilar said, "the fire just burst across the rugs and the records in the record player went up, poof, like an explosion . . ."

By now the first of the seven fire engines that responded to the alarm was roaring up the street with its siren wailing. Neighbors awakened. One of those was Mrs. Webb Overlander, wife of John Wayne's veteran makeup man who was also in Japan with the Duke. The Overlanders lived in a cottage near the Wayne house.

"I was horrified," Mrs. Overlander recalled. "Flames were shooting out all over the second floor. It was like an explosion. I thought they all were still in there."

Another petrified onlooker was Mrs. Donald LaCava who had rushed over from her own house nearby, along with Robert Morrison, another neighbor who was a movie producer—as well as Marion Michael Morrison's younger brother.

Terror gripped everyone as they watched the flames leap in the black night sky.

"Where are they?" Mrs. LaCava began to cry. "Where are they . . . ?"

More engines were on the scene now and firemen were playing streams of water on the blazing house.

Suddenly Mrs. Overlander caught sight of some movement in the kitchen area. "There . . . there!" she pointed. "They're coming out!"

Pilar, with the baby bundled in a blanket in her arms, came out first, followed by the maids and the small boy, Blackie, the hero dachshund, and two other dogs.

With tears in their eyes, Mrs. Overlander and Mrs. LaCava embraced Pilar. Mrs. LaCava took Aissa from Pilar, for she could see how distraught the Duke's wife was. As Pilar gave the baby to Mrs. LaCava, she felt a pain on her right elbow.

"You've been burned," Mrs. Overlander said.

"I don't remember it happening," Pilar said. "I didn't feel anything until just now."

Morrison escorted the women to Mrs. LaCava's house and, while Mrs. Overlander watched Aissa, Mrs. LaCava called a physician who came over, treated Pilar's elbow, and gave her a sedative.

It took the firemen more than an hour to put out the fire. By then the entire second floor was a smoldering ruin and the first floor had been severely damaged by smoke and water. Many valuable antiques and expensive personal belongings were also destroyed, along with the furnishings— but a priceless collection of John Wayne's movie mementos were saved by the firemen in a ground-floor den.

The damage to the house ran approximately $500,000 and it took months to effect repairs.

The day after the fire, Mrs. LaCava went to see a doctor herself. The visit had nothing to do with the fire. She had been experiencing certain discomforts which she suspected meant only one thing, and the physician merely confirmed it.

Mrs. LaCava was going to have a baby.

And what has that got to do with the story of John Wayne?

Only that she is the former Toni Wayne, Duke's daughter—and that her condition presaged the fact that John Wayne would nine months hence be a grandfather!

Toni had been married in one of Hollywood's most spectacular weddings of 1956, held in Blessed Sacrament Church, with the archbishop of Los Angeles, James Cardinal McIntyre, performing the ceremony, which was followed by a nuptial Mass.

More than 500 guests—including Bob Hope, Anne Blyth, and Loretta Young—were at the wedding, and the big guy was a typical father-of-the-bride before entering the church. He smoked incessantly, laughed nervously, fumbled numerous times with the bride's veil, and ran his fingers over his perspiring face.

As he paraded up the aisle with his lovely daughter on his arm, he looked as proud as a peacock. After the ceremony, Duke relaxed and enjoyed himself at the reception in the Crystal Room of the Beverly Hills Hotel.

Toni had dropped out of her last year at Immaculate Heart College in Los Angeles to marry Don, the nephew of famed movie director Gregory LaCava. Don, who had attended Loyola University with his bride's two brothers, was studying law and had served as a Navy aviator in the Korean War. They honeymooned in a favorite Wayne haunt—Acapulco.

Well, it may have been due to the fire. And Pilar was ready to concede that at least it had something to do with moving back into their rebuilt house that following September. It was a Saturday and the temperature in Encino was almost like it was back on the Morrison homestead on the edge of the Mojave Desert some forty years before.

At any rate, Duke and Pilar had a tiff.

It was serious enough for Big Duke to announce for all the world to hear:

"Pilar and I can't seem to get any warmth and understanding between us anymore. It's been coming for some time. I suppose it will end in divorce."

Pilar's complaint:

"Unfortunately, business is sometimes more important to a man than his wife. How can a wife live with a man who, after four years of marriage, spends two-and-a-half years on location. When he does get back from his movie-making, he spends all his time on business affairs."

Wayne didn't fault Pilar for her complaint. If anything, he seemed to agree with her.

"Yeah," he said when advised about his wife's statement, "maybe I talk about my business too much. And then when I'm making a picture I'm gone for three or four months at a stretch."

The next day, they were both singing a different tune.

Pilar: "Saturday was a hot day and we were moving and, well, I'm Latin and I sometimes explode, you know."

Wayne, pleased as a cowpoke home on the range, said: "Everything is okay now. We had a tiff and it looked like we were going to separate. But we've reconciled and I'm glad.

Almost a month to the day later, on October 7, 1958, John Wayne, was holding Angie Dickinson in his arms and telling her how much he loves her in a scene for *Rio Bravo*.

At that very moment he became a grandfather.

Toni gave birth to a seven-pound girl, named Maria Antonia (Mama's given names in reverse order), in St. Joseph's Hospital, where two years before her stepmother brought little Aissa into the world.

Eight months later, Big Duke became a grandfather for the second time when Alicia Marie was born to son Michael and his wife, Gretchen—and this is positively the last time we are going to try to keep track of the births of John Wayne's grandchildren.

At the end of this book we'll try and give you the latest total, but don't count on its accuracy. The whole thing is just too much to keep up with or to handle in one volume.

Meanwhile, John Wayne finished *The Horse Soldiers*, in which he was once again directed by John Ford, and began to work on a film that had been his dream for at least fourteen years.

CHAPTER XIV

The Alamo

The Alamo, a story of raw courage, dramatizes one of the greatest chapters in American history.

John Wayne was willing to bet $12 million plus Davy Crockett's coonskin cap and flintlock rifle on its success. Few people believed he had a chance to bring that kind of a picture in as a winner. Yet he was willing to bet everything he had and everything he could promise—his fortune, the fortunes of friends, his career, and his hopes—on this one motion picture.

For ten long years after the formation of his production company with Robert Fellows, Wayne had sought backing for this film. It was to be an emotion-packed, historically accurate account of how some 180 Americans, dug in at the historic mission in San Antonio, Texas, under the command of Colonels William B. Travis, James Bowie, and Davy Crockett, held out for thirteen days (February 23 to March 6, 1836) against a force of 4,000 Mexicans led by Antonio Lopez de Santa Anna, the dictator of Mexico. About 500 of the attacking force were killed. But a breach was made in the walls, and in the final assault, the Mexicans overpowered and slaughtered the garrison in a hand-to-hand struggle in the chapel.

"Remember the Alamo" became the war cry of the Texans, who under Sam Houston at San Jacinto six weeks later —on April 21, 1836—defeated and captured Santa Anna.

The Alamo was not to be just a Texas picture. It wasn't just another Western. It was a picture about the universal fight for freedom, with some of the rawest, bloodiest, and most savage adventure action ever filmed.

Since Wayne had a contract to do films in conjunction with United Artists, there was a moderate response from the company's executives—but their initial investment was not nearly what Wayne needed to make the picture.

Wayne estimated the film might run in the $6 million to $8 million neighborhood, which was rich for any Hollywood investor's blood, even by 1960 standards. This estimate would soon prove to be too low, but United Artists did come up with some money and with this backing Wayne was in business.

As producer and director, Wayne assigned the role of James Bowie, the dedicated cynic who commanded a force of volunteers inside the mission, to Richard Widmark.

Laurence Harvey was given the role of Colonel Travis, the aristocratic lady's man who was the arrogant but able commander of the army.

General Sam Houston, who later fought and won Texas's

last battle for independence, was played by Richard Boone.

Flaca, the woman who begged to die with her man, was played by Linda Crystal.

Joan O'Brien played the role of Mrs. Dickinson, who was spared by the ruthless Santa Anna and allowed to walk through the columns of Mexican soldiers with her daughter.

Singer Frankie Avalon had the role of Smitty, a messenger sent through enemy lines for help that never came.

And John Wayne's role was that of Colonel Davy Crockett, soldier and ex-Congressman from Tennessee, who rode 1,500 miles on horseback to get in on the fightin', some of the lovin', and a lot of the thinkin'.

Even Patrick Wayne had a significant part—Captain James Butler Bonham.

And Michael was working beside his dad as an assistant producer.

The locale for the filming of *The Alamo* was Brackettville, Texas, which lies some 100 miles west of San Antonio and just east of the Rio Grande and the Mexican Border. Since Brackettville had a population of only 1,858, supplies for this gigantic production became an immediate logistical problem—after the first and foremost problem of finances had been solved.

Wayne intended to follow history as accurately as any Hollywood producer-director had ever done. A good deal of manpower and material were needed for this portrayal of the story of the Alamo and Jimmy Grant, who once worked as a Chicago newspaperman and had since written scores of film scenarios, supplied the first material for the picture. It was the product of nine years of research into the lives of Davy Crockett, Jim Bowie, Bill Travis, and other Alamo immortals who loved life but hated tyranny more.

Al Ybarra, the art director of Batjac, supplied set designs and location plans based on eight years of his own research on the Alamo.

Casting director Frank Leyva and his associate, Tom Rosselle, then were given the task of solving the logistical problem that faced Wayne once everything else was ready —getting manpower and materials to the location. Leyva and Rosselle visited nearly every town in southwest Texas to recruit the army of 4,000 who were to enact Santa Anna's hordes attacking the Alamo.

Production manager Nate Edwards and unit manager Tom Andre performed one of the most monumental jobs in film history. They rented and/or bought 1,500 horses for the cavalry and then made arrangements for their housing and feeding.

The task of costuming the players and the thousands of extras fell to Frank Beetson, who had to supervise the accurate production of no less than twelve different types of gaudy uniforms worn by Santa Anna's forces. He saved $3,000 by installing drawstrings instead of zippers in those Mexican army uniforms—a tribute as well to Frank's sense of history. For who ever heard of zippers in 1836?

Head wrangler Bill Jones traveled 35,000 miles buying stock, including Texas longhorn cattle, by now a near-extinct breed.

Retired Marine Corps Sergeant Jack Pennick, a hero of the 6th Marines in the World War I battle of Belleau Wood, drilled the 4,000 members of Santa Anna's army to charge with real bayonets fixed on actual flintlock rifles. And fifty gunsmiths kept the rifles in firing order (it cost $1,500 every time a full volley was fired).

Of all the logistical problems in the production, however, the food-handling was the most complicated, not only from the standpoint of cost but in regard to preservation and preparation. Huge walk-in refrigerator-freezers had to be shipped to Brackettville and erected near the mess tents and kitchens. Not to mention the cooks and waiters and other help that had to be brought there to handle the feeding of so many people.

Rolly Harper, a former police lieutenant in Burbank, California, who had built a hotdog stand into a giant movie catering concern, had the task of serving more than 4,000 box lunches plus 800 hot lunches in the field on big-scene days. Total cost of feeding the cast, crew, and extras during their eighty-one days in Brackettville: $250,000.

Meat servings alone totaled 40,000 steaks, 14,000 pounds of roast beef, 14,000 pounds of ham, 4,800 pounds of sausage and bacon.

The special music for the picture, which of course was dubbed in Hollywood as the takes of the film were rushed there from location, was composed by Dmitri Tiompkin, who by that time had won four Academy Awards and was due to win others in years to come—but no Oscar for *The Alamo*.

Makeup supervision was handled by Web Overlander, whose wife you will remember was one of the concerned watchers at the Wayne house fire. Web, who'd been with the Big Duke for eighteen years and was by now one of his "inner circle," supervised scores of assistant makeup men who had the task of muddying faces with the red dust of battle and adding numerous other realistic touches to faces and bodies before any scene could be shot.

It took eighty-one days, as we said, to shoot *The Alamo*. When it was finished, and John Wayne was finally able to shout those happiest of orders on a set, "Cut! Print it!," the ulcer that had started to gnaw at him back in 1947 when he first sat behind his big executive's desk at Republic Pictures, was tormenting him as never before.

Wayne had gone through a "living hell" on this picture. For almost from the mid-point of production, funds started to get low. Costs ran ahead of the budget and Duke had to scrounge for more backing. United Artists came through with additional funds but not early enough to meet the spiraling costs that the picture was incurring. The big guy had to beg, borrow, and charm every penny that ultimately added up to the $12 million investment that went into *The Alamo.*

In doing so, Wayne also tapped his own reserves—so deeply, in fact, that everything he owned—the hotels, cotton plantations, oil wells, uranium mines, real-estate subdivisions, ice cream plants, that factory making sugar sacks in South America—everything, was mortgaged to the hilt. But Wayne didn't mind. He had produced the most lavish picture in all Hollywood history (*Cleopatra* cost $23 million at a later time but was filmed in Europe), and it was, bar none, the gaudiest by any standard.

"When I say we spent $12 million I'm leveling," Wayne said on a day not long before the film was premiered. "I've got everything I own in it. I borrowed from banks and friends. Take a look at one scene and you'll never be able to count the thousands of people."

Then he added what amounted to his unqualified confidence in the film's success.

"I'm not worried in the least bit," he said. "This is a darned good picture. It's real American history, the kind of movie we need today more than ever. It'll make money for years to come."

The picture made money but not on its first go-round of theaters—and not for Wayne. At least, not the kind of profits he had hoped would cascade into his now-empty money vaults. In time, he broke even—but only years after, when he sold a large hunk of his own interest in *The Alamo* to United Artists. By then, John Wayne had foundered on the verge of bankruptcy and literally had to start amassing the fortune he now has from scratch.

To say *The Alamo* was not an artistic success would be a gross error, for it won nearly a dozen Academy Award nominations—though not a single Oscar. However, as is so often the case with movies whose lavishness drives their producers to the precipice of financial disaster, *The Alamo* lacked virtuoso performances.

John Wayne, for instance, who had worked with John Ford so often, seemed to lack Ford's agility and pointedness as a director, and John Huston's sumptuous characterizing. *The Alamo* was rich in detail and strenuous in its decorative authenticity—including the $1,500,000 reproduction of both the Alamo and San Antonio, circa 1836—but it was like a too-rich mixture that had not been stirred and homogenized into one blend.

The battle scenes were remarkable. They leaped off the wide Todd-AO screen with the bodily energy of the 4,000 charging troops, and there was clear evidence that considerable ingenuity was employed to marshal all those extras into a stubbornly superb composition of action. Here was where Wayne's direction stood at its best. The spectacular falls from horses and from the walls of the Alamo gave the scenes breathtakingly visual excitement.

But there was a tendency to overdo oration, to spell out too distinctly and too dramatically certain sentiments of patriotism and religion that might best have been left seen and not heard. There was a looseness and wandering in the effort to bring the diverse elements of the story together in some relationship to their relative importance on the scales of history.

This was not another Western. It had the basic structure of a significant historical film, but it lacked the force that its many elements could have delivered to the screen if the whole had been put together more painstakingly.

When he visited the location during filming, John Ford, who had little if anything to do with the production, said:

"It's timeless. It's the greatest picture I've ever seen. It will run forever."

Ford also had a number of opportunities to view the "rushes" after they were printed. It's regrettable Wayne didn't also invite his friend to the cutting room. Some severe editing by Ford on the three hours and seventeen minutes of the finished film's running time might have made the screen version of *The Alamo* as historic as the battle itself.

The Alamo was also notable for the film debut of little Aissa Wayne, now four years old. Aissa played the daughter of Colonel Travis's captain of artillery, Almeron Dickinson, enacted by Ken Curtis, and she handled her role exceedingly well. Her most dramatic portrayal was in the exodus from the Alamo after its fall. Little Miss Wayne fled astride a mule—in all the 127 pictures he had made up to then, her daddy had never ridden such a humble four-legged critter.

The Alamo was to have been John Wayne's answer to Clark Gable's *Gone With the Wind.* But thirty-five years later, GWTW had still not been shown on TV and was still making periodic rounds of the theaters with all the fanfare and box-office tariff of a first-run film. *The Alamo* became a "casualty" of TV in September, 1971—only eleven years after its release.

If *The Alamo* served no other purpose, it did at least add another significant chapter to the legend of John Duke Wayne.

CHAPTER XV

Duke as a Salesman

Even as the dust of the battles of *The Alamo* was still blackening the skies and the thunder of flintlock rifles were crashing deafeningly on the Brackettville plains, John Wayne was stirring up the nation's patriotic consciousness with a double-page spread in *Life* magazine. It combined a drum-roll for the forthcoming $12 million epic and a commentary on American politics.

"A statement of principle," written by Duke's publicist, Russell Birdwell and signed by John Wayne, tied *The Alamo* to the current political scene. The Democrats and Republicans had drawn their battle lines for another kind of Alamo. John F. Kennedy was making an assault on the GOP bastions which had been defended for eight years by Eisenhower and had now been turned over to Nixon.

JFK was about to adopt the title of a 1935 John Wayne movie as the rallying cry of his Administration—*The New Frontier.*

"There Were No Ghost Writers at the Alamo," read the headline over the text. When Wayne was asked why he had spent $152,000 for an ad to vent his political beliefs, he replied:

"Because I'm an actor I don't think I should be robbed of the right to speak. I hoped that by taking out the ad this way I might prompt more motion picture companies into taking out institutional ads with a more patriotic attitude in their text. It seems to me we are limited now to a few television announcers and an occasional newspaper writer to remind us that we owe a little something to our country rather than what our country owes us in federal relief insurance, old age health and welfare benefits, and the like.

"Speaking as a citizen of the U.S., as a guy at the corner drug store, I think politics today is smothering the individual principles of candidates who are all bounded by party rules so it would be very pleasant for me to find a man, a Republican or Democrat or whatever, who really speaks up and says what he thinks.

"In delving back into the history of the time of the Alamo I found that men still in their twenties thought deeply of the problems of our country. They were the men who gave us our heritage and I don't think we give our heritage enough careful thought. Days are moving too fast. We don't sit down and think of the real purposes and needs of our existence.

"I think we need to reflect on our history—to realize that when we are aroused we can be savage and cruel and that in time of need we can carry our share of burdens as we are proving to the tune of some $70 billion of foreign aid each year.

"Now with the political conventions upon us it behooves us to choose a leader—a man who can stand up and tell us what he thinks is right whether it works a hardship on us or not. We need men who will recall to the world what we Americans really are."

This says it better than the text of the ad in *Life*—because this was John Wayne and not a publicist talking.

Was it eccentricity, megalomania, or simply just pure honest conviction that he could arouse a citizenry to its obligations as Americans that prompted John Wayne to be so outspoken?

One of Wayne's critics happened to be a magazine writer named James Heneghan, who offered this view of Duke:

"Wayne likes to believe that he is relentlessly honorable and that his word is his bond. This is not true, anymore than it is true that any man is entirely honorable. He would like to be in life a John Wayne character in a movie, but he has never quite made it.

"His ambition is well-buttressed by an almost egomaniac belief in himself. On one occasion, this writer was riding with him in a plane over southeast Asia. The drone of the motors dulled our senses and we sat quietly making small conversation.

"Apropos of nothing, except possibly that he had just finished a movie for which he had been paid $1 million, I said, 'Duke, when you were a kid did you ever think that when you grew up you'd be the No. 1 movie star of the world?'

" 'Hell, no,' he said. 'I thought I'd be President of the United States. I didn't see how I could miss.' "

Heneghan, who had known Wayne and worked for him as a writer for some ten years, was no longer associated with the Duke. There'd been a falling out just before *The Alamo* went into production. Heneghan sued Wayne for $102,500, claiming he was promised $100,000 for helping Duke arrange financing for the picture, but that all he got paid was $9,000. In addition, Henaghan asked for $11,500 for other work performed. The suit was settled out of court without disclosure of details.

The set-to with Heneghan wasn't Wayne's only encounter with trouble during 1960—problems with *The Alamo* aside.

Did you ever hear of Duke's square-off with Frank Sinatra?

It all apparently started over Frankie's disagreement with Wayne's public opposition to the hiring of Albert Maltz, one of the so-called Hollywood Ten, to write a screenplay for *The Execution of Private Slovic.* Sinatra had been criticized widely for hiring Maltz, who had been jailed in 1951 for refusing to tell a Congressional committee whether he had been a Communist.

Frank eventually succumbed to the pressure and let the blacklisted writer go. But Frank was sore at Wayne, who had beaten the drums the loudest for Maltz's firing.

You may find it hard to believe, but Sinatra was dressed like an Indian squaw and Wayne in cowboy gear when they had their encounter in the Moulin Rouge on Hollywood's Sunset Boulevard. The occasion for their presence at that spa was a $100-a-plate dinner for the benefit of SHARE, the organization which aids mentally retarded children.

Sinatra arrived at the affair in a Rolls-Royce belonging to Sammy Davis, Jr., accompanied by Sammy, who came as a

Confederate soldier, and by Dean Martin and a non-member of the Rat Pack, Milton Berle.

After Wayne went on-stage and sang "Red River Valley" and Frankie followed with "The Lady is a Tramp," the two came face-to-face as they were about to leave the nightclub.

Duke gave Sinatra a friendly "hello" but there was no cordiality on Frank's part.

"You seem to disagree with me," Sinatra said in answer to Wayne's greeting and started to argue Maltz's cause.

"We can discuss this somewhere else," Wayne said, but Frankie just kept arguing and then, finally, stepped in on the Duke—all five-foot-seven and 150 pounds of him. Sinatra, who knows how to handle his *dukes,* would have been hard-pressed to handle this *Duke*—standing six-foot-four and tipping the scales at 225 pounds. He might have chipped a piece of the granite forming on ol' John's face— if he could have reached that far with his fist. But after that . . . well, Frank could always count on his good pals, Sammy and Dean, to give him splendid last rites.

Fortunately, no call had to be made for the mortuary wagon. Friends stepped in and separated David and Goliath before any blood was spilled. Wayne headed for his car and Sinatra did likewise, but then something happened in the parking lot.

Perhaps because of all that excitement, Frankie stepped in front of a Thunderbird driven by lot attendant Clarence English and almost got run over. English jammed on the brakes and brought the car to a screeching halt scant inches from the terrified Sinatra.

The twenty-year-old English was more in Sinatra's height and weight range. Frank stormed to the driver's side, stuck his hand into the car, and tore the attendant's shirt trying to pull him out. Another attendant, Edward J. Moran, twenty-one, came over and said, "Aw, Frank, he wasn't trying to hit you with the car . . . He's only trying to make a living."

Sinatra turned to Moran glaring. "Who the fuck are you?" he demanded. Then he pushed Moran away. But Moran surged back and clouted Frankie with a right cross that stunned him. Moran was coming over with another punch when a six-footer, weighing about 220 pounds, and later identified as one of Sinatra's bodyguards, stepped in, hurled Moran against the car, and began pummeling him. Two other parking lot attendants pulled the man off Moran, who had to be taken to Hollywood Receiving Hospital for treatment of bruises he suffered on his left temple and ear.

Later, Moran signed an assault complaint, naming Sinatra and a "John Doe" as his assailants. Police also said that Sinatra had been drinking.

Still later, Sinatra denied that the guy who slugged Moran was his bodyguard. "I don't have bodyguards," Frankie insisted. "And I'll pay $10,000 to any newspaperman or anyone else who can prove that I have or ever had a bodyguard."

Nor was that all that happened during the period. When John Wayne's troubles with the preparation and shooting of *The Alamo* were snowballing, this also took place:

La Jean Ethridge, twenty-seven, was a beautiful movie starlet. One of the extras in Wayne's $12 million picture, she had come down to Brackettville with the rest of the cast and crew and went to live in a bunkhouse in nearby Spofford. Her roommates happened to be five men, also extras. One was Chester Harvey Smith, thirty-two, who apparently became La Jean's lover.

After filming began, Duke was so taken by the starlet's execution of the small part she'd been given that he decided to elevate her to a featured role. That evening, La Jean went to the bunkhouse and began packing her things. She was going to move out and take quarters in Brackettville—but no one has ever said exactly where.

But this much is fact: Wayne upped her salary from $75 to $350 a week.

When Smith came home and saw his sweetheart putting her clothes into a suitcase, he demanded to know where she was going. They had lived together for four weeks. She told him what she was doing and he flew into a rage. There was a long argument. Finally, Smith grabbed a bowie knife and plunged it into La Jean's chest. She collapsed and soon died in a pool of her own blood.

Kinney County sheriff's deputies arrested Smith and charged him with La Jean's murder after he told them:

"I couldn't stand being without her . . ."

Five days later, an examining trial was held by Justice of the Peace Albert Postel in the quaint little Brackettville Courthouse. Reporters probably would not have gone near the court except for one dramatic turn. San Antonio attorney Fred Semaan was retained by Smith to represent him. Almost at once the lawyer served a subpoena on Wayne to appear as a witness at the hearing.

On the day scheduled for the examining trial, reporters from various newspapers and wire services came to the courthouse—only to find that Postel had ordered a closed hearing. That meant press and public were barred. Great mystery suddenly descended over the case. No one could understand why Postel had decided to issue that order.

There were protests from Wayne's Texas attorneys who had come to Brackettville to be with him. State's Attorney

Leon Douglas warned that such a closed-door proceeding might be contrary to state law. Postel said he would assume the responsibility for his action and stood on his original order.

The defendant's attorney, Semaan, also voiced a strong protest to the kind of trial dictated by Postel.

"I don't know what they have in mind, but I aim to find out," Semaan said. "One minute this thing's open, the next thing it's closed tighter than a bank on Sunday. If they're trying to hide anything, I'm going to find out. Maybe there's nothing to it, but I'm going to raise a lot of hell finding out if there isn't."

No amount of hell that Semaan raised changed the judge's position. The examining trial was held—and it was closed.

The first witness called by the court was Art Names, an official of a repertory group of which La Jean and Smith were members. Names entered the courtroom at 9:30 A.M. and remained inside until almost noon.

The next witness was a tall, bruiser of a man wearing a big white hat, red shirt, tight-fitting Western trousers, and boots. He was recognized by everyone because he was John Wayne. He was inside only a few minutes. When asked what testimony he gave, Wayne replied:

"I am bound by the court's order not to reveal what I said . . ."

Later Kinney County Prosecutor John Tobin said that the hearing had been closed by Postel "because of the intimate testimony given by Mr. Wayne and the four men who lived in the same house with Miss Ethridge."

I covered the story at the time for the *New York Journal-American*—by telephone. I called the Brackettville district attorney, Douglas A. Newton, who made the request for the closed testimony to Justice Postel. I wanted to find out the reasons behind the action.

"Go to hell," Newton said to me. "I ain't talkin' to you or anyone else. I have my reasons." And he hung up.

One of the curious aftermaths of the case was that there never was an aftermath. Nobody followed the case. Nobody tried to find out what had happened in the courtroom that day. But when I got to writing Big Duke's biography, I felt that I ought to do a little diggin' to learn what I could. So I called Chester Harvey Smith's lawyer, Fred Semaan in San Antonio, and asked him to bring me up to date.

A trial was held in Brackettville but no jury was needed. Smith pleaded guilty and was sentenced to twenty years. After doing about seven and a half years, Semaan said, Smith was paroled.

"Now can you tell me what happened that day at the closed examining trial?" I asked Semaan. He roared with laughter as he began to tell me.

"John Wayne wasn't a witness to the killing, but I wanted him on the stand to tell us that because this girl was dead they were going to have to shoot a lot of scenes over again. And for that reason, either he or his company apparently were putting pressure on the D.A. to push the case harder than he should have.

"When he was served with my subpoena, Wayne called me and threatened not to come. And I told him, by God, if he didn't he'd get thrown in jail. So when he did come . . . I don't know anything about him, but I can be pretty nasty . . . I began calling him John *Payne* on the witness stand, deliberately.

"Payne was then playing in something they called *The*

Left-Handed Gun and when I called Wayne 'Mr. Payne,' oh, did he get indignant.

" 'I'm not Payne, I'm Wayne,' he protested.

" 'Oh, I beg your pardon, Mr. Wayne,' I said. Then a few minutes later I'd call him Payne again and he'd blow up again. After a while I got to saying to him, 'Now Mr. ah ... let's see now, are you Payne or Wayne, I can't remember . . .'

" 'I'm Wayne!' he shouted at me.

"Well, when the hearing was over ... but before that let me tell you what my first impressions of him were. You know that he barged in there like a big bear. Everyone on the set, I'm sure, was kowtowing to him. He thought I was going to. He didn't mean a damn thing to me. Just another witness ... so we walked outside when the hearing was over and he was pretty nice about it.

"I thought he was coming over to give me some trouble and I was getting ready for it. And he walked up to me and then he began to grin. He says to me, 'You kinda poured it on, didn't you?'

" 'Yeah,' I said to him, 'you kinda asked for it, didn't ya?'

"He says, 'Yeah, I guess I did.' So we shook hands and we ended up good friends."

Semaan said he understands Wayne's early obstinance.

"I could see his attitude, first calling up and saying, 'I'm not coming,' and then when I got him on the witness stand being half-haughty . . . That came from his being accustomed to giving everybody orders . . . And I don't take orders from anybody. I cooled him off pretty quick by making him pretty hot. That's the way to handle guys like that . . ."

Not all Texans were as tough on Big Duke as the five-foot-three lawyer from San Antonio. The governor of the Lone Star State, Price Daniel, was far more cordial. He invited John to the big, new Houston Music Hall to accept a plaque as the "Outstanding Texas Salesman of the Year."

That was the livin' end—John Wayne, a Texas salesman.

CHAPTER XVI

Revolt in Panama

After *The Alamo*, John Wayne kept his commitment with 20th Century-Fox by making the second of his three $666,666.66-salary films for them—and, boy, could he use that money! The picture was *North to Alaska*, with Henry Hathaway directing and Stewart Granger, Capucine, and Ernie Kovacs in strong supporting roles. Then followed Duke's final contractual obligation to Fox, *The Comancheros.*

Wayne was now free to answer another call from John Ford who wanted to direct him in *The Man Who Shot Liberty Valance*, over at Paramount. For the first time in his career as a superstar, Wayne was teamed at last with an actor who possessed every bit of his stature; indeed, a man who also had his longevity and in the eyes of many was a better actor --James Stewart.

Even as Wayne was involved in these new films, he couldn't avoid getting entwined in still another imbroglio. It was getting to be Academy Award time again and, as it had become the custom in recent years, everyone—from song writers to actors—was taking out ads in the Hollywood trade papers trumpeting his own horn for nomination.

One such ad was in the name of Chill Wills, who played the beekeeper in *The Alamo*. Wills, in fact, went so far as to circularize voting members of the Academy of Motion Picture Arts and Sciences, besides running numerous ads asking his "cousins" to vote for him.

His continual reference to "cousins" prompted Groucho Marx to take out an ad which said: "Dear Mr. Chill Wills, I am delighted to be your cousin but I voted for Sal Mineo."

Mort Sahl was so impressed by Groucho's ad that at a Screen Writers' Guild dinner he suggested a new Oscar be awarded to Groucho for "the best ad for nomination for an Academy Award."

The comic-opera flavor of *The Alamo* campaign was further enhanced when Russell Birdwell, Wayne's publicist, bought four full pages in each Hollywood trade paper and chastised two local motion picture critics who'd chastised Birdwell for his extensive and expensive publicity and ad campaign for *The Alamo*.

Birdwell seemed especially put out about a paragraph written by film critic Dick Williams which said: "The implication [of Birdwell's *Alamo* ads] is unmistakable. Oscar voters are being appealed to on a patriotic basis. The impression is left that one's proud sense of Americanism may be suspected if one does not vote for *The Alamo*. This is grossly unfair. Obviously one can be the most ardent of

American patriots and still think *The Alamo* was a mediocre movie."

Charge followed countercharge. The real casualty was Chill Wills, who apparently knew nothing about the controversial ad in his name. His press agent had done it without advising him.

Wayne didn't even know that when he decided to step in with his own full-page ads in the film capital's trade papers, wherein he blasted poor Chill for his "bad taste" and called him to task for placing one particular ad which read:

"We of *The Alamo* cast are praying harder—than the real Texans prayed—for their lives in the Alamo—for Chill Wills to win the Oscar . . ."

Later, when asked for comment, Wayne replied:

"No one in the Batjac organization or the Russell Birdwell office has been a party to Mr. Will's trade-paper advertising. I refrain from using stronger language because I am sure his intentions were not as bad as his taste."

Joe Hyams, the well-known Hollywood columnist, had this final word on the rhubarb:

"The battle between Messrs. Wayne and Wills seems to be a high point in the Hollywood battle waging around *The Alamo*, which threatens to make the original scrap look like a skirmish. There are those in Hollywood, including this writer, who think that for Mr. Wayne to impugn Mr. Wills's taste is tantamount to Jayne Mansfield criticizing Sabrina for too much exposure."

The ones put out most of all by this give-and-take were the members of the Academy, who were so concerned about the out-of-hand campaigning for nominations that they were considering banning any type of promotion in the future by aspirants for Oscars.

But all the ads that were taken out might just have been a waste of money because *The Alamo* had suddenly gotten itself several million dollars worth of free publicity in the most expensive medium of all—television. The American Broadcasting Company, which had sent camera crews to Brackettville, presented an hour-long TV spectacular based on the filming of *The Alamo*.

When Wayne was first approached by ABC-TV with the idea, he couldn't believe his ears. Duke had never had thoughts of going on TV himself, although many of his earlier oaters were being screened on the boob tube almost nightly. But this chance to show the country a bit about his extravagant production—well, that was something else again. Wayne closed down his own filming of the picture for two whole days while the ABC camera crew moved in and shot the footage.

A short time later, Wayne was off for Africa to do another film for Paramount, Howard Hawks's *Hatari*. When the film was finished, a *Hatari* safari was organized with the film's stars—Wayne, Elsa Martinelli, Hardy Kruger, Michele Girardon, Red Buttons, and Bruce Cabot—who went on a ten-city cavalcade promoting the picture. The caravan included a menagerie of wild animals, including Sonya the cheetah, who appeared in the film.

Pilar visited her husband in Africa during the filming of *Hatari* and brought Aissa along this time. But Pilar couldn't stay long. She was pregnant and there was no telling when John Ethan Wayne, the name his parents had decided to give the baby if it was a boy, would make his debut.

It happened on Washington's Birthday, February 22, 1962, a short time after Duke returned from Paris where he had appeared in a cameo for Darryl F. Zanuck's production of *The Longest Day*. Like Aissa, John Ethan was born in St. Joseph's Hospital and he weighed in at eight pounds two ounces. It was a joyous occasion for both Pilar and Duke. During a pregnancy two years before, Pilar had suffered a miscarriage in her fifth month. Although her gynecologist had assured her that she could continue to bear children, Pilar was beset with doubts. With John Ethan's birth, those apprehensions were dispelled.

We deliberately delayed talking about one other significant earlier happening in John Wayne's life because so much other hell was breaking loose around him at the time. In 1959 the Duke became embroiled in a revolutionary plot centering around his old pal, Roberto Tito Arias, down in Panama.

Arias, who had served his country as ambassador to Great Britain, slowly but surely came under suspicion of building up an effort to overthrow Panama's government. When the Panamanian authorities went in search of Arias, they couldn't find him. But they seized his wife, ballerina Margot Fonteyn, and took her in for a night of unpleasant questioning in Panama City.

Margot insisted she didn't know where her husband was hiding and when the authorities released her she quickly fled to New York, hoping Roberto would get in touch with her there. Meanwhile, National Guard troops were put on the alert to prevent the overthrow of President Ernest de la Guardia. One unit of troops camped on the beach along the Santa Clara coastal area to defend against a possible "invasion."

In the middle of the night, the guardsmen captured a suspected rebel wading ashore. Questioning revealed he was one of ten men—led by Arias—who had landed with a

supply of arms from Argentina. The guardsmen were led
to a spot on the beach about seventy-five miles west of
Panama City and dug up a cache that included seventeen
pistols, a .30-caliber machine gun, a rifle, and 1,000 rounds
of ammunition.

Santa Clara was also the site of Arias's family estate and
that fact, after the arms cache was found, prompted the
troops to raid the grounds in their search for the fugitive.
They didn't find him, but they uncovered some documents
in his beach cottage. One of these papers was a letter dated
April 12, 1959, addressed to Arias with the signature
"Duke Wayne."

Attached to the letter was an interoffice memorandum to
Wayne from Robert D. Weesner, one of Duke's aides, listing funds involved in business transactions with Arias.

According to the memo, Arias had been given or had
drawn against Wayne's account a total of $525,000 since
November 19, 1957. The big question that the Panamanian
authorities now asked was: Had John Wayne been sending
money to Arias to support a revolution in that country?

At home in Encino, Wayne said he was "really shocked"
by the reports of Arias's revolutionary activity. "I've known
Tito for twenty years on and off," Duke said. "I've got
business in Panama with him and without him. I also know
other members of the family."

Wayne went on to explain his business ties with Arias.

"It's a shrimp company business—not just he and I.
Other people are in it. But he's a big stockholder."

Authorities investigating the landing of the arms on the
Santa Clara shore learned that a shrimp boat had figured
prominently in that venture, which tended to throw added
significance to the Wayne-Arias business alliance and the

$525,000 that Duke had sent to Tito over an eighteen-month period.

But a few hours after Wayne was implicated in the plot, Panamanian officials cleared him.

"We are satisfied," a spokesman for the President said, "that Mr. Wayne was in no way connected with the attempts to overthrow the Government. His deals with Arias were strictly business . . ."

It was a great relief to John Wayne's millions of fans and to his associates that his involvement with Arias was in business and not revolution. Big Duke, who in his time had fought off howling bands of Apaches, brought down all the beasts in Africa, outwitted some slower-witted Russian spies, thwarted Mongol hordes, swapped punches with the toughest Irishman in County Galway, sloshed ashore at Iwo Jima, suffered through and survived countless travails in the Canadian wilderness, piloted an entire Chinese village through the Formosa Straits, brought in an ailing airliner with a smile and a whistle, defended the Alamo, and—what the hell, there didn't seem to be anything that John Wayne couldn't do.

But Wayne lead a revolution in Panama—an honest-to-goodness, real-life revolution?

Never, never, never!

It was indeed a great relief to learn that there was nothing fishy about Wayne sending those half-million fish to Tito Arias. It was strictly for the shrimps.

But there did come a time when Wayne watchers became a bit disenchanted with their rugged hero. It happened when he was filming *Donovan's Reef* in late August, 1962, and . . .

Remember, if we failed to mention it so far, Big Duke had

never let a stunt man take his place in even the roughest scenes in his movies. He always did the scenes himself. One thing that John Wayne could never be accused of being is a sissy.

Well, on that *Donovan's Reef* set that day, Wayne was in front of the cameras with Lee Marvin in a knockdown, drag-out nightclub fight scene. Duke, now fifty-five, was supposed to take a rap at Lee—after Lee first swung at Duke. Marvin carried through with his assignment. Following the script, John started to fall backwards. He was supposed to land against a real, hard table. But some boob had put a Hollywood table in its place—a prop that falls apart at a touch.

Big Duke landed on that table and to everyone's utter horror he crashed to the floor.

"Cut!" cried John Ford, who was directing this one, too. Ford knew this scene wasn't in the script. And he could see the grimace on Big Duke's face.

"Are you all right, Duke!" Ford asked.

"Yeah," Wayne snorted, his craggy, weather-lined face contorted in pain. "I'm okay."

"Where does it hurt?" Ford wanted to know.

"On my ass, if you really wanna know," he said.

The Paramount flack promptly reported the accident to the press and quoted Wayne as saying:

"I hurt my back . . . it was an old back injury. Hurt it horseback riding. I'll be all right."

(I happen to have been the Paramount flack who wrote the release on that movie. It happened during the big newspaper blackout of 1962–63 when all six of New York City's papers were on strike. Paramount called me and wanted to know if I would do some publicity for them—and I did.)

Ford ordered Duke to go home and shooting was suspended the rest of that day.

"Don't worry about me," Wayne said as he left. "I'll be back . . ."

And he was the next day. The scene with Lee Marvin was finished. This time they put the right table in place for John to fall against. But the unscheduled scene of John Wayne crashing to the floor—did they scrap that? Not on your life.

"It was the best shot in the whole picture," Ford said.

Donovan's Reef was a significant film only because of what it stood for in those early years of the 1960s. To begin with, the brawling between Wayne and Marvin was in the John Ford tradition, one of the most cinematically stylish ways ever devised. It may have been a couple of decades stale, but nobody has yet found any other way to stage a fight on the silver screen.

But what was happening in movies now was that there was a trend away from action pictures—he-man action, that is. Even that isn't precisely what we really mean. Or what Wayne was trying to say. Let Duke say it:

"Ten or fifteen years ago, audiences went to pictures to see men behaving like men. Today there are too many neurotic roles . . . It's the Tennessee Williams effect both on Broadway and in movies . . ."

Some so-called intellectuals may have been inclined to dismiss Wayne as a nice guy but no ball of fire in the I.Q. department. But the big guy was no dope. The wheels were clicking all the time—and when Wayne opened his yap, a lot of people listened. And still do.

That's what bugged "intellectuals" who were making their assault on the film capital, taking over movie studios lock, stock, and barrel, and putting out their pornographic pictures under the label of "art."

"Williams and a lot of other writers go far afield to find American men who are extreme cases," Wayne said. "They aren't representative of the average man in this country, but they give the impression that we are a nation of weaklings who can't keep up with the pressures of modern living."

Wayne, of course, was disqualified automatically—by his very appearance—from playing the kind of roles that were being given to Tony Perkins, Anthony Franciosa, Rod Steiger, Paul Newman, and other "sensitive" types, the "new breed" of Hollywood actors.

Not only couldn't Wayne play their roles—he wouldn't. He would rather be found dead than portray those trembling, torn T-shirt types.

So far as John Wayne was concerned, many of the film capital's new heroes were nothing but zeroes.

CHAPTER XVII

In Harm's Way

Being married to Pilar and having two children gave John Wayne the kind of home life he'd never been able to experience before. After the fire, their house was completely redecorated. Pilar carried through much of the original theme that Chata had employed, but there were significant changes in the motif which reflected many of her own tastes.

The living room was the most imposing part of the house, with the fieldstone of the outer wall carried inside to shape the huge fireplace. At one end of the living room, Pilar put a valuable collection of authentic prints of Indian life, an oversized billiard table, and a hi-fi set concealed in an antique phonograph.

Duke had his own den-office, an extra large room with a

198

small fireplace, a deep red rug, and amber-colored draw curtains. His trophies, his gun collection, and his Kachina dolls, made by the Pueblo Indians, were all displayed in his den.

"When Duke thinks," Pilar said, "he uses his den to pace back and forth."

Another room that was strictly Duke's was the gym upstairs where he would exercise every morning and work up an appetite.

"He's a discouragingly early riser," Pilar explained. "He attacks a dainty breakfast of steak, eggs, toast, grapefruit, and coffee. Duke simply loves steaks for breakfast, lunch, and dinner."

After the fire, Duke had the den restored and installed facilities which converted the room into a movie theater, complete with a projection room and a screen which disappeared into the ceiling.

"On Saturdays and Sundays we like to have friends in to dinner, and afterward he runs films well into the morning," Pilar said about Duke.

What kind of movies does Wayne show the visitors?

"He likes Westerns, of course," smiled Pilar. "I like Westerns only when John Wayne stars in them."

That's the way a large segment of the movie-going public has always looked at it, too.

One day in 1963, for example, around the time that Wayne had taken Pilar and Aissa off on location to Nogales, Arizona, to do *McLintock*, an enterprising newsman named Hyman Goldberg, writing then for the old *New York Mirror*, went on a tour of Los Angeles with a producer and counted the number of theater marquees proclaiming one or another of John Wayne's latest movies—they tallied nine!

At about this same time, Frank Sinatra stood on the podium at the Academy Awards banquet and bore down heavily with the point that he was sick and tired of people in and out of the movie industry discussing interminably the question: What is wrong with the picture business?

Frank's solution, one of hundreds suggested, was to make better pictures.

"There's nothing wrong with the movie industry," said the producer who went on the tour of L.A. with Goldberg. "Nothing that couldn't be cured by a dozen John Waynes."

But there was only one John Wayne and no one could expect him to make more pictures. No actor in Hollywood had worked more industriously or more strenuously than Big Duke for the past thirty-four years. He was now well into the second half-century of his life and his sixtieth birthday was only four short years away. Yet he was giving up nothing. He was prepared and determined to make picture after picture so long as he could stand it.

Throughout all those many years, he had exhibited a remarkable endurance, and, even more remarkably, he had seldom been sick for more than a day of his life. That ulcer had been annoying, but Wayne knew how to cope with it. Whenever it acted up, he'd put the Scotch bottle away and wait to take that drink—or two, or three, or more—another day.

But on location for *McLintock*, Wayne noticed something that was not anything like his past experiences with minor ills which decked him, at most, a day or two; ailments like the flu, a touch of the virus, or the grippe.

This was different—he was coughing. He had had this problem for several months. He thought it might have been from too much smoking—Duke had always been a five-pack-a-day man. So he cut down on cigarettes. But the cough persisted—and worsened.

Pilar became so concerned about him that she told her husband he ought to see a doctor.

"Awww, it'll go away," he dismissed her.

But he also promised Pilar that he'd see a doctor after they returned home from Nogales. Duke had other things on his mind, more important to him than his health—he had to make a movie.

The film, about a reactionary old cattle baron coping with encroaching homesteaders, discontented Indians, a marriageable daughter, and a rebellious wife, is the story of McLintock, played by Wayne himself. Maureen O'Hara played McLintock's wife, and when it came to a sparring partner for the Big Duke in a battle of the sexes, no one ever approached the vigor of this redhaired beauty.

Miss O'Hara provided some of the lustiest farce, particularly in a scene in which she is dunked in a mudhole in the film's funniest brawl, and a finale in which she flees Wayne down Main Street in her underwear. Standing on the sidelines were such strong supporting performers as Edgar Buchanan, Stephanie Powers, Yvonne DeCarlo, and—Chill Wills. Yup, ol' Chill, who'd been reprimanded by Duke for his "bad taste" campaign to get himself an Oscar, had been forgiven and was playing in another Wayne epic of the frontier.

This picture was more of a family affair than any of John's past films. Not only did Patrick have a featured role as Devlin Warren, but Aissa also had a good part and son Michael again worked as an assistant director. But not behind his father this time because Duke didn't direct. That's what made it such a big family affair. Andrew V. McLaglen,

Victor's son and Duke's old friend, was running this show. Andy, who'd made hundreds of TV Westerns, principally *Have Gun, Will Travel* and *Gunsmoke*, had practically grown up in Duke's household.

When young McLaglen was casting for talent for *Gunsmoke*, he offered the role to Wayne before snaring James Arness.

"I turned it down," said Duke. "If I had appeared in a filmed TV show it would have been too diminutive for me and would probably hurt my movie image."

Another interested onlooker during the shooting of *McLintock* was Pilar, who stayed on location almost the entire time that the picture was being filmed.

Victor McLaglen, of course, was dead by now. In fact, a number of John Wayne's closest friends or associates had died in the past few years. Ward Bond succumbed to a heart attack in 1960. Then Clark Gable went that same year just as he was making a remarkable recovery from a heart attack suffered after completing *The Misfits* with Marilyn Monroe. Then, within a year, Gary Cooper died of cancer . . .

When John Wayne returned home from Nogales, his cough was worse than ever but he still wouldn't go to the doctor. He had too many things to do.

He had signed for *Circus World*, a story that tells of the tour through Europe of Matt Master's Circus, a Wild West show of the 1910 era, and he was off to Spain for the filming. Wayne played Masters, and others in the cast were Rita Hayworth, Claudia Cardinale, Lloyd Nolan, Richard Conte, and John Smith.

In a scene that was being filmed in Madrid, director Henry Hathaway brought the actors under a tent to shoot a circus fire. The blaze, like all such incendiary scenes in make-believe, was to have been controlled—but it wasn't. An unexpected breeze set the flames blazing the wrong way.

Wayne, who on-camera was trying to put out the fire, suddenly realized what was happening. The flames began devouring the canvas. As players, technicians, and workers fled, Wayne made his way to safety with them. Minutes later, about forty square feet of the top of the tent collapsed. An elephant, a lion, and other animals had been moved just in time.

Firemen put out the blaze and Hathaway later confirmed what he suspected when he saw the rushes—the fire was bigger and better than the script called for.

The picture was unique for one other fact. Miss Hayworth, now forty-four, a sex goddess twenty years before, played the mother of Miss Cardinale, who at twenty-two was Europe's latest reigning sex symbol.

When Wayne returned to the States, he was still coughing, but he still was not ready to follow Pilar's advice and see a doctor. He was intent on keeping his commitments to play a featured role in *The Greatest Story Ever Told* and to star *In Harm's Way* for Otto Preminger.

Even then, however, there was another distraction to keep him from his date with the doctor. Melinda Ann Wayne was now twenty-three years old and she was marrying Gregory Robert Munoz, a twenty-six-year-old Los Angeles County deputy district attorney. The ceremony and nuptial Mass were held in Blessed Sacrament Church and Cardinal McIntyre performed the rites as he always had at the marriages of Wayne's children.

Seven hundred guests filled the pews. Among them were

such stars as Cesar Romero, Jeanne Crain, Irene Dunne, and an old friend, Loretta Young.

During the nuptial Mass, Melinda started teetering at her kneeling bench. Wayne, sitting fifteen feet away in his pew, saw his daughter in trouble and dashed to her side. He caught her just as she began to fall.

With Duke holding her on one side and the kneeling bridegroom on the other, the pretty brunette bride soon came out of her fainting spell. A priest brought a chair and she sat throughout the rest of the Mass.

Later, at the reception, John Wayne abided by the axiom propounded by his old friend, Toots Shor, the New York City nightclub owner and confidant of athletes and showbiz folks—"nobody who isn't drunk by midnight is drinkin' right."

And Wayne was still coughing . . .

He finally went to the Scripp's Clinic in La Jolla and X-rays showed a spot on his right lung. The doctors gave it to him straight—the spot looked like a tumor and it had to be removed. He was ordered into Hollywood's Good Samaritan Hospital immediately.

No flares were sent up when Duke entered the hospital in mid-September, 1964, but a few days later his son, Michael, made an announcement about his father's illness.

"Dad went into the hospital to have surgery on an old ankle injury. He had pulled an ankle tendon loose while making *Legend of the Lost* in North Africa in 1955 . . ."

This was pure bull. But Wayne had been scheduled to begin shooting *The Sons of Katie Elder* in a couple of months, and Michael really turned it on.

"With his new Western coming up with lots of horsebacking, the doctors advised him to let them tack the tendon down. After all, it had been a thing that had haunted him for about ten years. And you know, this is the first time he's ever been in a hospital in his life . . .''

Michael also told reporters that after the operation his father had suffered a "respiratory complication." That was nearer to the truth.

"It was an infection, an abcess of some kind," the young man said, "really one of those things that happens to you in hospitals when you're lying around and inactive. I just got out of the hospital myself with a broken leg, and while I was there I contracted gout and what they call a pulmonary embolism . . .''

Mike had been in an auto crackup with brother Pat a few months before.

The Duke, his son said, should be out of the hospital in a week.

But two weeks later, Wayne was still in the hospital and everyone was wondering what was keeping him there if he was convalescing only from ankle surgery and a respiratory infection. So James Bacon, the Hollywood reporter, went to see the Duke.

"I don't know what the hell I had but the Doc said whatever it was I licked it," Wayne stated. "I had a rough ten days in the intensive care unit. They kept bringing in all those cardiac cases besides me. Finally I told them to get me a gun. I was ready to shoot my way out."

Duke was moved to another floor.

Now came the first clue of Wayne's real trouble, since Michael was still giving everybody a snow job about his old man's true ailment.

"I had two operations in five days," Wayne told Bacon. "That was the rough part. First they took that *thing* from my lung. Then I got to coughing later, coughed so damn hard that I busted a tissue. So they had to open me up again . . ."

Michael put in that the *thing* was "an abcess of the lung."

No one wanted to tell the truth—not even Wayne. But the truth seeped out just a bit when Duke was discharged from the hospital on October 8. As he walked out into the bright sunshine, he told reporters:

"I had a chest tumor removed . . ."

"Was it cancerous?" someone asked.

"I guess not," Wayne replied.

The Big Duke went to his home in Encino and wasn't heard from again for months. When the time came to begin filming *The Sons of Katie Elder*, Henry Hathaway and Paramount had to put it off. Wayne couldn't make it. He was still convalescing.

At Christmas time, I called Wayne at home after Earl Wilson broke the story that Duke had licked cancer. I wanted to do Duke's own story for *Photoplay* magazine. And here is what the Duke told me:

"It was a tough operation. They had to take out the top of my lung and I lost a rib. Then they found that they had to yank me open again for edema after I swelled up like a puppy . . . it was the fluid collecting in my lung.

"But I licked cancer—the Big C as they call it. I caught it early. I was lucky. I hope my story will get other people out for checkups with their docs so that some poor soul can be as lucky as I was.

"I don't want to turn people's insides when I'm talking about it, but I've got to level with my fans. I don't want anybody to feel having cancer is like having leprosy. This is something you can talk about—and something you can beat.

"I beat it—because they found it early enough. All it took to tell them that I was in danger was an examination that showed a spot on my lung. That was all the warning I needed.

"The doc didn't try to hide the seriousness of the condition. He leveled with me. I understood what it was all about and I realized that I'd have to undergo that operation. I told the doc to go ahead.

"After they operated on me and took that thing from my lung, it looked like everything was going to be all right."

Wayne spoke about the operation with a casual air, as though it had been a scene in one of his movies.

"In any operation there's always the danger of complication—and it happened to me. While I was in the intensive care unit I began coughing. I coughed so much that I busted some tissue.

"To make matters worse, I developed an abcess which caused an abnormal amount of fluid to accumulate in the lung.

"Pilar said I swelled so much that I looked more like Sydney Greenstreet.

"The doc said I'd have to be operated on again. So they wheeled me back into the operating room and cut me open again. That was rough, too—a second surgery on top of the first, and all in the space of five days.

"They put me back in the intensive care unit and around this time I began to hope I had seen the last of the operating room. As the days went by I gained my strength back and I began feeling good.

"On my own in there, I would have been happy. But they have other patients in the hospital who need constant care as I did, and seeing them wheel the surgery and heart patients right next to me didn't help matters on my account.

"I began to squawk and tell them I wanted out. But they said I had to stay.

"Meanwhile, my physical condition improved rapidly. My appetite was great and they were letting me get a crack at some man-sized meals like soup, steaks, pork chops, salads, and all the trimmings. That, of course, was after I came off the intravenous feeding.

"It got so that the nurses would needle me about my appetite. I guess they hadn't seen big eaters before.

"But those surroundings in the intensive care unit were getting me down. I finally told them to get me my guns—I was going to shoot my way out.

"They got the message at last and I was moved to another part of the hospital. It was a nice private room with TV. That gave me a chance to see a lot of shows I'd been missing—practically everything except the old John Wayne movies.

"I caught Jackie Gleason's show, too, but he drove me nuts. I watched him lighting those cigarettes and I'd have to look away. I guess I don't have to tell you that smoking was out for me.

"And I was a five-pack-a-day smoker. For forty years I smoked five packs a day—and the unfiltered kind. Maybe you've seen me in the ads.

"That was my only discomfort—not being able to drag on those cigarettes. But I've begun getting used to being a non-smoker now. I won't touch them either. That's orders from the doctor.

"During my period of convalescence in the hospital, I was visited by Pilar, the children, and a great many friends. I was also interviewed by the press.

"Now they all wondered what it was I had. Some of them would ask Pilar what was wrong with me. I remember Pilar was quoted in the newspapers about my having edema and swelling up like Sydney Greenstreet. But she didn't tell anyone it was cancer.

"Michael described what I had as an abcess of the lung.

"As for myself, I had simply said that I didn't know what the hell I had, but quoted my doc as saying that whatever it was, I had it licked. That was the truth.

"Actually I wanted to tell everyone that I had cancer right from the start. I'm not the kind of guy who tells fibs. None of us do—to anyone.

"But my advisers, those fellows who worry about how my pictures are making out, pleaded with me not to tell anyone. They thought it would destroy my image.

"So we had to be careful how we answered people's questions.

"When they'd ask if I had heart trouble, the answer was no.

"When they'd ask if I had cancer, the answer was the same.

"And it wasn't lying. The truth of it was that I didn't have cancer—not anymore. The doc had assured me that they had gotten it all when they put me under the knife.

"It was lucky for us that nobody asked: 'Did he have cancer?' If the question had been put that way, I guess we would have had to answer with the truth. But no one had put it exactly like that.

"But as time went on I got to thinking about it. And I thought about all the unfortunate people who may have cancer and have no idea that they do. I thought how wonderful it would be if I could tell them how important a checkup is—how lucky I was that I found out about my condition in time. In time to save my life. In time to enable me to make a complete recovery.

"And I also thought about the people who know they have cancer and how fearful they might be of going under the knife. Or how they might live in dread fear that they cannot be cured.

"The more I thought about my own case the more I wanted to sound off and tell everybody how important it is to get a checkup with the doc. Even if my story helps just one poor soul into being as lucky as I was—then I'll consider this story to be worthwhile.

"You know, there are probably a lot of skeptics about this. They may say, 'How does he know the doc is giving him the straight dope?'

"Well, let me tell you. I faced up to the doc and put it squarely to him. I wanted the straight dope. I told him 'Don't lie to me. I want the truth.'

"All I've got to say is the doc knows me damn well enough to know he hadn't better. So he told me he got all of it because it was caught early.

"That's why I'm here telling the world I had cancer and licked it.

"I don't go by the Hollywood code that cancer or some other serious illness can destroy a box-office image. And I don't buy what my advisers said—that the public doesn't want its movie heroes associated with a serious illness like cancer.

"What I say is the public—the fans—want the truth. I say there's a lot better image when John Wayne licks cancer.

"I also think there's a lot better John Wayne now. I feel a lot better and look a lot better. I've always had to fight my weight, but being laid up as I was I lost enough pounds to put me in great shape for my next film, *The Sons of Katie Elder.*

"It's a typical John Wayne Western—plenty of action. I see by the script that I'm going to have to spend half the time in the water. It's a very rough picture.

"But I know I have to be healthy to be playing in it.

"And the doc will be checking me periodically to make certain that I stay healthy.

"I'm a lucky guy. I beat the toughest opponent I've ever known.

"I licked the Big C."

And that was Big Duke's story to me in 1964 when he had beaten the specter of death and rejoined the living.

CHAPTER XVIII

His Old Self Again

By February, 1965, John Wayne had not only licked the Big C but was ready to show the world that he was no cardboard cowboy. The crags and wrinkles now showed more than ever on his fifty-eight-year-old cheeks and forehead; his hair was thinner, his toupee larger, and the scars across his chest ached when the weather was damp. But he was back and was ready to make his 139th film, *The Sons of Katie Elder.*

Henry Hathaway called the Duke for a scene. The big guy adjusted his eighty-gallon hat, and lumbered toward the director with his lopsided half-grin and that curious pigeon-toed, high-shouldered gait. His eyes were squinting and he was happy, because he knew he was back and he had a picture that he could sink his teeth into. He was pleased also that Dean Martin was there, playing his gambling, carousing brother.

There were two other brothers, Earl Holliman and Michael Anderson, Jr., and all four converged on a Texas town for the funeral of their beloved "Ma," who had scrimped and saved to send her youngest son to college— after her husband was murdered with a bullet in his back.

The Texas country that film fans saw in the picture wasn't really Texas country. *Sons of Katie Elder* was filmed in dusty Durango, across the Mexican border, and the interior shots were filmed at the Churubusco Studios in Mexico City, which was rapidly coming to be known as John Wayne country.

In Mexico City they know him as Juan Juayne and they have been calling him *El Macho* ("the manly one") for many years. Wayne is a cowboy saint to the Mexicans and many of them are indebted to him for shooting so many of his movies there and giving their economy an uplift. The Mexicans make groovy extras—they roll cigarettes like cowpunchers from Dodge City and they can shoot it out like they mean it.

Wayne went through the filming as though he had never spent three weeks in the hospital and three months in convalescence. Only the portable inhalator that he had on the sidelines for a "lift" with a whiff of pure oxygen now and then in that 8,000-foot altitude gave any clue that the Duke wasn't his old self. Even the people with two lungs were having difficulty breathing in that rarified air.

One day in Mexico City, the renowned Dr. Charles W. Mayo, of the Mayo Clinic, went to visit John Wayne to congratulate him for doing "a wonderful job in combating the cancer phobia." The doctor, one of the world's leading cancer specialists, cited Wayne for his efforts to warn people about cancer and for saying that he owed his life to a medical checkup.

"When I tell someone they need a checkup," Mayo said, "they think I'm looking for business. It has a completely different effect when a public figure like Mr. Wayne says it."

Director Hathaway then came into the picture.

"I was operated on for cancer of the stomach in the Mayo Clinic twelve years ago," he revealed. "The cancer has not returned . . ."

Following *The Sons of Katie Elder*, Wayne headed for Italy to film *Cast a Giant Shadow*, which teamed him with Kirk Douglas, Yul Brynner, Senta Berger, and Angie Dickinson.

The filming was done at Santa Maria Galleria, thirty kilometers outside of Rome. There was a jeep scene—Wayne and Douglas fighting over Miss Dickinson. The brawl didn't last long. Suddenly Wayne cried out in pain.

It was his back. He was bundled into a car and driven to the nearby Villa Clara Hospital where X-rays showed he had suffered a slipped disc. He was confined to the hospital three days, then discharged with orders from the doctor to rest for three or four more days.

"Hell, I wanna finish and get home," Wayne told director Melville Shavelson. "Let's get on with the jeep scene."

Three days later Duke was on a jet heading back to the United States. But he stopped for a couple of days in London for a visit with his old buddy, Roberto Tito Arias. Tito was in the Stoke Mandeville Clinic in Buckinghamshire—a cripple ever since a political rival had fired four bullets into his back some two years before in Panama.

Wayne returned to California just in time to be near Pilar when she was ready to make her husband a proud father for the third time in his marriage to her, the seventh time all told. This time St. Joseph's Hospital was much farther from their home. Duke and Pilar had sold their big house in the

San Fernando Valley and had made their new address at 2686 Bay Shore Drive in Newport Beach.

Pilar gave birth to a six-pound fourteen and a half-ounce girl, as usual at St. Joseph's, because Pilar wouldn't have her babies any other place. It happened on February 22, 1966, John Ethan Wayne's fourth birthday—and less than three months away from her daddy's fifty-ninth birthday. The baby was named Marisa.

Marisa made her entrance as her father began filming his one hundred forty-second movie, *El Dorado*, a Howard Hawks Western with the Big Duke paired with bow-legged Robert Mitchum in a plot that sees them brush off all the villains without a single casualty for our side—except for a bullet hole Duke suffers at the base of his spine, and another inflicted on Mitchum. It was a Western in the Wayne tradition.

And then came *The War Wagon*, pitting Wayne against another strong man, Kirk Douglas, who'd costarred with him in the roughhouse, *Cast a Giant Shadow*, which featured the jeep fight that sent John to the hospital.

War Wagon was also filmed in Mexico among the real tumbleweed of the Durango country, and it was notable for one particularly touchy episode involving Kirk and Duke. At the time, Ronald Reagan was running for his first term as governor of California. In the middle of production, Douglas went off to make a TV spot *against* Reagan. Wayne was infuriated.

"Well, I fixed old Cleft-chin," Wayne snickered. "I halted production on the picture while I went off and made a trailer *for* Reagan—and Kirk had to stay on the set to wait for his call."

What particularly irked Wayne at the time was that so

many members of the Hollywood colony had gone out of their way to make TV political commercials "demeaning actors running for governor, and at the same time demeaning their own profession."

There was more to Wayne's and Douglas's rivalry on screen in *War Wagon*, such as when Kirk bests Duke in springing onto his horse. Wayne leaped into his saddle like Wayne always did, but Douglas sprung so high he cleared two horses entirely and landed on the far side of both on the ground. Of course, what the movie audiences didn't know was that Kirk had trampolened the distance.

A good laugh came when Wayne and Douglas joined forces to kill a pair of gunmen coming at them. Having shot them down, Duke and Kirk argued about their skills.

"Mine hit the ground first," said Douglas.

"Mine was taller," said Wayne.

Wayne thought the picture was good enough to win an award, but it didn't. Later Duke lamentfully gave his thoughts on why his films had never been given honors. Speaking about *War Wagon*, he said:

"Cannes wanted this picture but the studio was chicken. I never had a chance in a festival and there went my chance for glory. But at least I could always say I had two Academy Award nominations for *She Wore a Yellow Ribbon* and *Sands of Iwo Jima*."

There he goes again. Duke, you never got nominated for *Yellow Ribbon!*

"I'm not hurt and I'm not angry," Wayne continued. "I'm aware that I'm unpopular in the industry because my political philosophy is different from the prevailing attitude in the business. But I don't reply when they gang up on me because I think political streetfighting is unprofessional.

"It makes me feel lost to watch these people letting these things happen to them. Why don't they fight back? I'll tell you this, the pendulum's gonna swing the other way. Ask those damn liberal actors and actresses what they pay their servants. I'll bet I pay mine better."

Duke Wayne was now approaching his sixtieth birthday. He would soon be incurring the enmity of many more people because of his political stance and his ideas of what a man must do to be a patriot.

It all came out of a seventeen-day trip he made in the early summer of 1966.

CHAPTER XIX

Superhawk

Back in 1960 when he was busy making *The Alamo*, when he was trying to convince attorney Fred Semaan that his name was Wayne and not Payne, and when he was getting a plaque from Governor Price Daniels as "Outstanding Texas Salesman of the Year," John Wayne also went to a Gridiron dinner and met the Lone Star State's senior senator, Lyndon B. Johnson.

Sometime in early 1966, while still doing *El Dorado* for Paramount, Wayne read Robin Moore's *The Green Berets*, a novel based on the fighting of the U.S. Special Forces A-team in Vietnam. The book was a best seller and Wayne, enthralled by the story, saw an opportunity to do what no other Hollywood producer had dared to do—make a picture about the Vietnam fighting.

218

Wayne met resistance everywhere. Two major studios—Columbia and Universal—considered the project too costly. Wayne suspected that it would be nearer the truth to say that the subject was too risky for them. As he was well aware, at least three other film-makers had shelved plans to make Vietnam movies.

"This stuff about an unpopular war," Wayne scoffed. "Well, what war was popular?"

Wayne was supremely confident in his ability not only to make this a patriotic film—but a big money-maker as well, which is the first consideration in any negotiation with a prospective backer.

"I didn't think there was any doubt about this picture making money," Wayne said. "My record was pretty good. An awful lot of these fellas know how to talk motion pictures, but Goddamn few of them know how to make them."

He desperately wanted to make the picture, for he had promised the boys in Vietnam he'd do it when he visited the warfront in June, 1966, on a USO handshaking tour.

While with the 7th Marine Regiment near their base at Chu Lai, Wayne was signing autographs when suddenly several rounds of rifle fire tore up the dirt about fifty feet away. Wayne looked around with a grimace at the edge of the jungle from where the shots had come, turned, and snarled, "The yella bastards do all their shootin' from hidin', don't they?"

Then he went on signing his name on the helmet of a young marine. A security squad went after the sniper but found only an abandoned bicycle.

Before leaving, Wayne promised the marines that he would let "the American people know what's going on over here."

Wayne finally found Warners, now combined as Warners-Seven Arts, willing to listen. And willing to invest $7 million. "But," as Wayne put it, "I had to make a lot rougher deal than I would normally have made." Translated this means he wasn't going to profit as handsomely from his work as an actor and director as he had on other productions. Since he was well into the 90 percent tax bracket, it mattered little to Wayne.

The book was bought for about $50,000. The next step was to line up a cast and find a location suitable for recreating the frightful jungle scenes, the sickening sights, the terrifying sounds, and the other horrors that were Vietnam. Wayne considered several locations, but each posed a technical problem. Where would the tanks, guns, helicopters, and planes come from? They'd have to be supplied by the military.

Duke struck upon an idea—write to LBJ, who, since that Gridiron dinner in 1960, had changed his address to 1600 Pennsylvania Avenue, Washington, D.C. Duke got the letter off in December, 1966. In effect, what he said in his note to the President was:

"I'd like to make this picture about the boys in Vietnam. Is there going to be cooperation or not?"

The President's press secretary, Bill Moyers, wrote back that Johnson was interested in the project and that it sounded like an exciting venture. Moyers turned the Duke over to the Defense Department, which immediately assigned Major Jerold R. Dodds, a young Green Beret, to serve as the first of several technical advisers for the film.

Incidentally, when Moyers wrote to Wayne, he didn't say anything about LBJ being mad at the Big Duke for stumping for Barry Goldwater in the 1964 Presidential race.

Wayne wanted to shoot the picture where the real action was—in Vietnam. Eyebrows were raised in the Pentagon, and even in Moscow. The newspaper *Sovietskaya Kultura* ("Soviet Culture") assailed Wayne for wanting to film in the fighting zone. It called Duke an extreme reactionary and said:

"He might find himself in the path of real bullets if he goes ahead with his plans to shoot a movie about the Green Berets in Vietnam. He is trying to glorify the heroic deeds of these insidious, specially taught soldier-killers.

"Mr. Wayne's previous films have been shot in the completely safe prairies of Texas or the hills of Colorado where his heroes play out their game by firing at dummy targets. He will find real bullets if he goes to Vietnam."

The Pentagon told Wayne that it was not a good idea to make the film in the war zone and set out in search of an alternate site, promising to find one.

Duke began casting and his choice of stars was made, he said, without regard to their off-screen feelings about the war. He wound up with a cast headed by David Janssen, Aldo Ray, Jim Hutton, Raymond St. Jacques, and Bruce Cabot.

"The viewpoints among the people I signed for parts in the picture ranged from the concurring to the pacifist," Wayne said. "But I didn't give a damn how they felt about the war, so long as they knew what to do before the cameras."

A location was finally selected for the film. It was the Army's sprawling Fort Benning in Georgia. After filming got under way on August 9, 1967, it quickly became apparent that this production might turn into another *Alamo*. Production costs ran ahead of the budget, but what was even worse—Wayne was falling far behind schedule.

Warners-Seven Arts, which was not unaware of what had happened down in Brackettville when no one rode herd on Wayne, sent one of its most experienced directors to "help out." Mervyn Le Roy, who directed such masterpieces as *Thirty Seconds Over Tokyo* and *Mister Roberts*, and more than seventy other films, arrived in a fur-collared coat, puffing on a big cigar.

"Duke," he said, "I don't aim to get in your way . . . but I wish ta hell you'd hurry things up and get this show on the road."

"Just stay outa my friggin' way," Wayne growled. Then he smiled at Le Roy, shook hands, and said, "I know why you're here, Merv, and I ain't bitchin' to *you*. I know it's those Goddamn stock manipulators at the studio. If I stand still a minute, they think there's nothin' to do. Well, the truth of it is I had an eye infection and I had to shoot a few close-ups around me, so they send you here . . ."

Later Wayne and Le Roy had a few rhubarbs on their own. One explosion came when Wayne, as Colonel Kirby, was playing an office scene with a Vietnamese officer. Le Roy suggested master coverage with the camera, followed by cuts of the individuals. Wayne doesn't like master scenes (filling the frame with everything).

"That's old-fashioned," Wayne protested. But he relented finally, saying, "It ain't important enough to raise a fuss."

Although Wayne did most of the directing, Le Roy and Ray Kellog (who worked on the night scenes) were also given credits for directing. But Wayne never found it difficult directing *himself* in scenes, although he'd only done it once before—in *The Alamo*.

The Duke was a tiger when he was running the show at Benning.

"Okay, roll 'em!" he'd roar with a fierce glare. Then he'd shout, "Action!"

Black smudge pots sent up smoke, rifles crackled, grenades exploded, bodies dropped, soldiers groaned in agony as they were hit by "bullets" and "shrapnel," and all together the scene became one of scores that were to recreate the sickening sights, terrifying sounds, and other horrors that were the Vietnam War.

When Wayne was satisfied that the camera had caught all the action and drama, he'd yell, "Cut! Cut!" And then he'd shout to the players, "Just ga-reat, folks!"

The shooting at Benning lasted 107 days and it involved an expenditure of something like $45,000 a day, much of it allocated for special effects, eighteen high-priced stunt men, 1,500 black-powder bombs (six times the number used in the average war movie), a ton of dynamite, about 60,000 rounds of small-arms ammunition, plus gasoline and diesel fuel.

As it was, the film's cost would have been considerably higher had it not been for the military establishment's generosity.

"The Army provided certain things that were not readily available," explained Captain August Schomburg, Jr., who'd been assigned as the project officer for the movie.

Le Roy put it more bluntly:

"You wouldn't get these planes and these choppers and these soldiers and everything around here unless they wanted this picture made."

Oh, yes, the soldiers. Wayne had been given carte blanche to use as many soldiers from the base as he needed, provided they worked during their own leave time. They were paid extra's wages—$1.40 an hour, or $100 a week if used full time.

Other military personnel, such as Captain Schomburg and Major Dodds, were detailed to the movie set from their usual duties, while still others, such as the platoon of Hawaiians flown down from Fort Devens in Massachusetts (to appear as Vietnamese and Vietcong) were on administrative leave—which meant taxpayers' time.

And there was a sequel to this situation, as you will see in a moment . . .

The shooting was not yet over on the one hundred and seventh day, November 15, 1967, when a freak of nature suddenly ruined what few days were left for finishing the film at Benning. A premature frost transformed the leaves of the "jungle" to autumnal foliage. This necessitated the construction of an expensive twenty-acre jungle in Hollywood to finish the remaining scenes.

The picture was finished at a total cost of approximately $8 million—a million more than Warners-Seven Arts had budgeted—and it was released to wide critical acclaim but much wider criticism. Wayne had expected nothing less, nothing more. But at least he had kept his promise to the G.I.s in Vietnam. He had done something at home to let the folks know what was going on over in that part of the world.

The Green Berets grossed somewhere in excess of $12 million, which more than justified the investment—and more was to be made as the film went on a rerelease to theaters, then ultimately to TV. But it also drew unexpected flak from Washington long after the movie had been screened around the world.

Representative Benjamin S. Rosenthal, a Democrat from New York City's borough of Queens, took John Wayne to task in mid-1969 for what he charged was the Army's "subsidization" of the production, because they had supplied men, equipment, and assistance for the film.

Rosenthal made public a General Accounting Office report showing that the Army had charged Batjac $18,623.64 for services provided during the 107 days of filming at Benning. The GAO is the government's auditing branch, yet Rosenthal claimed that it had been unable to calculate the complete cost of the government's aid to Wayne in making the film.

"Some people have suggested $1 million," Rosenthal claimed. "Maybe it should be more than that." The congressman then catalogued the lengths gone to by the Army in its efforts to help in the production of the film. He cited the use of Fort Benning, The two officers (Major Dodds and Captain Schomburg), eighty-five hours flying time that had been logged in an undesignated number of UH-1 combat helicopters, the use of M-16 rifles, 81-mm. mortars, M-60 machine guns, M-78 grenade launchers, bulldozer cranes, trucks that were put at Batjac's disposal, and the contribution of 3,800 man-days by the Army in support of the film.

Wayne, who was on the West Coast when the congressman fired his broadside, stood up to the attack.

"The Pentagon was more than careful in billing us," Duke said. "The $18,623 was not a token payment but the exact amount for government equipment we couldn't get elsewhere. Moreover, we spent $171,000 on the base in building a camp they used after we left, out in the undeveloped boondocks. We in no way interfered with their business and we never used one military person if he was on duty.

"We paid $305,000 for extras for seventy days of actual shooting, and 80 percent was for off-duty military personnel and their families. We also paid our room and board expenses."

An Army spokesman said the department felt it had been properly reimbursed for assistance to *The Green Berets* and added:

"We charged for what they used."

Rosenthal, who asked the House Government Operations Committee to investigate motion pictures made with assistance from the Defense Department, fired one last shot at Wayne before the whole matter faded away like most political typhoons generated by oratorical downdrafts.

"The glorified portrayal of the Vietnam War, which is the heart of the film, raises serious questions about the Defense Department's role in using tax funds for direct propaganda purposes," the congressman cried.

Wayne got in the final word. He accused Rosenthal of seeking publicity and belittling "one of the only films I know about that's expressly been making Americans appear heroes around the world."

Wayne expressed some of his other views also:

"If they would call this a war, the American people would get behind it, I think. Semantics again. Things that we know would be absolute treason during a war. They can do that now and get away with it because they can be covered by words in the Supreme Court for any goddamn thing they do.

"Like marching, and carrying the Vietcong flag. I think they oughta shoot 'em if they're carrying the Vietcong flag.

A lot of our boys are getting shot lookin' at that flag. As far as I'm concerned, it wouldn't bother me a bit to pull the trigger on one of 'em.

"I have seen what's going on over there, and I have seen the guns and ammunition that our boys are getting killed with. Well, it's a Communist conspiracy, and there it is . . . As far as I'm concerned, they are our enemy. The Communists are our enemy, not the Russian people. The Communist conspiracy is our enemy.

"If you go into any depth on it—the war—it has to be almost that you're for it; if you're a decent person you can't let people be so oppressed, particularly when you've told them and the rest of the world that you'll stop it. Which we have been doing since 1917; telling them that and not doing anything about it. Well, we did it in World War II; we tried. We lost the peace.

"The only way Vietnam could bring on a third world war is if Russia figures they can't win the world any other way. What the hell—they're gradually taking over weaker nations, pushing their leaders out windows, and finally crushing them after they win their own freedom, like in Hungary. That should have started a third world war. We'd been telling the people, 'Stand up for your rights and we'll back ya up.' We've been doing this for years, and it's about time we kept our word . . ."

Someone once said, "If you have a message, send a telegram."

Western Union has been on the skids for years because of people like the Duke. When John Wayne has a message to send—he makes a movie.

Pow! And Randolph Scott looks like he's about to lose his suspenders after a crack on the jaw from Big Duke in *The Spoilers* (1942).

It's getting to be a habit. Randy's getting another going over from John, but this is another picture, *Pittsburgh* (1943).

Victor McLaglen, Duke's off-screen buddy, tries to comfort an old soldier on his last day in the cavalry, from *She Wore A Yellow Ribbon* (1949).

This battle between Victor and Duke ranged all over the Irish countryside. Despite such violence the picture was called *The Quiet Man* (1952).

Banzai! Victor Sen Yung is about to get a bayonet in the gut for toying with Lauren Bacall in *Blood Alley* (1955).

Here's *The Man Who Shot Liberty Valance* (1962).

Duke leads the cavalry in *The Horse Soldiers* (1959).

John Wayne may look like a dentist in this scene but what he's really trying to do is extract his thumb from Lee Marvin's toothy grip in *Donovan's Reef* (1968).

Drift back through the years now that we've gone through John Wayne's life in pictures. The grizzled saddle-tramp looks like he could have played Rooster Cogburn, too. It's almost as if John Wayne, at twenty-two, is seeing how he will look some forty years hence. That's Tyrone Power Sr. being stared down in *The Big Trail* way back in 1930.

Marshal Rooster Cogburn is felled by booze in Academy Award-winning style in *True Grit* (1969).

CHAPTER XX

The Political Animal

I remember the night very well. A Thursday. I'd just returned home from bowling. It was June 20, 1968. My wife reads a great deal and she was absorbed in the *New York Times* when I walked into the bedroom, stripped to my underwear, and crawled under the sheets of our king-sized bed in Melville, Long Island. I was sound asleep in seconds.

Something like two hours later, around 2:00 A.M., my wife shook me awake. She always does when she spots something shocking in a newspaper or magazine, and what she had just read prompted her to say:

"My God, if the *New York Post* is supposed to be a liberal newspaper, what is the *Times*?"

"Way, way to the left," I said. "All their editors are Commies. Now let me sleep."

"No," she insisted. "You've got to read what they said about John Wayne's new movie . . . you'll never believe it."

"Good," I said, "anything they say about him is okay by me. You haven't forgotten how he wrung my neck, have you?"

"But this is terrible," she persisted. "Even *you* wouldn't have written such a harsh story about him . . . please, wake up and read it . . ."

I knew I wouldn't have any peace, so I took the paper and squinted at the story through half-closed eyes. The first paragraph not only popped my eyelids open but, as Wayne had said when he saw Chata's doodles about Nicky Hilton, made me want to vomit. It was the most vituperative and vapid volley of vocabulary I'd ever read. And I quote:

"*The Green Berets* is a film so unspeakable, so stupid, so rotten and false in every detail that it passes through being fun, through being funny, through being camp, through everything and becomes an invitation to grieve, not for our soldiers or for Vietnam (the film could not be more false or do a greater disservice to either of them) but for what has happened to the fantasy-making apparatus in this country. Simplicities of the right, simplicities of the left, but this one is beyond the possible. It is vile and insane. On top of that, it is dull . . ."

That was the first paragraph. The first sentence had seventy-three words, and if anyone had written a run-on of words that long on the old *Journal-American*, City Editor Edward A. Mahar would have taken the culprit into the men's room and kicked him in the groin. I'm not sure what he would have done to Renata Adler, who, I might point out, no longer works for the *Times*, but the point I'm trying to make here is that the times they are a-changing for a lot of movie critics. American movie-goers are disenchanted with the personal viewpoints of many of these writers, which all too often color their critiques. And realizing that they no longer influence the judgments of the movie-going public, these critics abandon good taste in their analyses and become "stupid . . . rotten . . . vile . . . and insane . . ." themselves behind their typewriters.

Sophistication and intelligence in America are at an all-time high and are still rising to new plateaus. Movies that are cursed and panned by critics mint grosses of $12 million for Hollywood—because fewer and fewer people are paying attention to what the critics are saying. Americans can spot propaganda in their newspapers as readily as they can detect it in a Kremlin communique.

"*Green Berets*, Rapped as 'Vile, Insane' Film, Is 'Boffo' at Box Office."

That was the headline in the *Wall Street Journal* about a fortnight after the rap in the *Times*, which was quoted in the story, as was *Newsweek*, which also panned the film, although not nearly so vitriolically. What really counted was what the financial and business world's most respected organ had to report about *Green Berets*:

"Despite what appears to be critical overkill, the film-going public is marching to the beat of a different drummer —to box-offices across the country . . ."

In its first week, the showbiz world's own *Variety* reported, the film grossed $71,000 in a Chicago theater and $56,000 at Warners' Broadway Theater in New York City. It was this newspaper's headlines of "Whammo" and "Boffo" that the *Wall Street Journal* was quoting.

Even the *Post*, which I consider (despite John Wayne's views) a mirror of honest reporting and a reflector of fair comment, was judicious in its review of *The Green Berets* despite an editorial stand wholly opposed to our involvement in Vietnam. Its ace movie critic, Archer Winston, wrote:

"People who are against the Vietnam war will consider this picture vicious propaganda. People who are for it have a choice. They can consider the picture a rousing war tale in the John Wayne muscular tradition or a solid blow for our side.

"Physically and in the action, there is a basic appeal. Georgia's Fort Benning sandhill country serves pretty well as a location for the advanced camp fighting. The personnel and materiel are certainly there in sufficient force. It is the kind of film that's out of style at the moment, but it's probably not nearly as bad as some folk will think, say and write, though some of its familiar sentimental and dialogue gambits leave it open to ridicule."

Isn't that more the way a movie critic should do it?

By early 1969, the *Times* was "marching to the beat of a different drummer" and clarioning a different tune. Now they saw "fit to print" this news about *Green Berets*:

"John Wayne, who lost the first battle, has won the war as usual," wrote movie critic A. H. Weiler.

"*The Green Berets*, his controversial film about the unresolved seven-year American involvement in Vietnam, opened last June to a barrage of negative reviews, and is turning into one of the most successful movies released by Warner Brothers-Seven Arts in the last five years. It has earned, up to now, nearly $11 million."

Then Wayne was quoted:

"I think those terrible reviews helped us a great deal. I've been in this business for forty years and any statements I've made in movies have been pretty truthful, I think. When people read those reviews I'm sure they couldn't believe them . . . *The Green Berets* simply says that a lot of our brave guys are fighting and dying for us out there. The ridiculously one-sided criticism of the picture only made people more conscious of it and they are proving that the reviews were not very effective."

Perhaps the whole thing was put in proper perspective by Michael Wayne, who said:

"Most critics reviewed the war and not the picture, which is about people, not politics. It certainly portrays Americans as heroes and it shows that moviegoers were ready for American hero images in this war."

During the summer of 1968, John Wayne went into production on his one hundred forty-fourth picture, *Hellfighters*, again directed by Andy McLaglen for Universal, but the Big Duke had other things to think about now.

The Republicans were holding their twenty-ninth National Convention in Miami Beach and Wayne had been invited to address the delegates. Wayne was the eighteenth of twenty-one speakers at the opening session in Convention Hall and his talk had been billed as an "inspirational reading." But instead of choosing a piece to read, he decided to speak about what he wanted for his daughter.

Wayne was introduced by William Murfin, chairman of the Florida delegation, who went to the microphone and said: "I present to you a man who is a giant of the screen and is, first, last, and always an American."

The band in the rear of the auditorium struck up "You Ought to Be in Pictures" and Wayne, smiling broadly, walked through the blue curtain behind the platform dressed in a dark blue pinstriped suit. For the first time since the beginning of seventeen speeches which preceded Wayne, the delegates quieted down and began to pay attention.

"Took me a long time ta decide to stand up here," he began. "I'm about as political as a Bengal tiger."

At ease on the lectern, Wayne told his listeners that he couldn't see the teleprompter without his glasses—nor did he have a script. He was speaking from the heart.

"I've read some reviews by my left-wing friends," he said, referring to the criticism of The Green Berets. Then he told the delegates and the millions watching on TV:

"I'm here because this is the party that cares. To use a good old American phrase, this party gives a damn . . . I feel the nation is more than a government, it's an attitude. Dean Martin asked me what I wanted for my baby girl when she was born. I gave him my answer. It was on Election Day and the bars were closed and Dean had time to listen.

"I told him I wanted her to get a good start in life—get some values that some articulate few say are old-fashioned —and most of all, I'm grateful for every day I spend in America . . ."

The delegates cheered and applauded and the band broke out with "You Ought to Be in Pictures" again.

"I know this may sound corny," Duke went on, "but the first thing I'm going to teach her is the Lord's Prayer."

More applause.

"And I don't care if she doesn't memorize the Gettysburg Address, but I want her to understand it."

Wayne wound up by saying that his daughter won't have to raise a hand to defend her country but "I'm gonna make sure she respects all who do."

He left Convention Hall under another hail of applause,

signed some autographs outside, jumped into a car, drove to the Fontainebleau, and headed straight for the bar where he ordered a fast screwdriver.

"I'm here because this party is the only thing wakening to the needs of the country," Duke said. Tony Martin, who was standing next to Wayne, nodded in agreement. Someone asked Wayne what was wrong with the country.

"Well," he began, his back resting against the bar rail, "I think we've been a little permissive. A little about time to be concerned about what the fella next door is doin'." He paused, shook his head, and muttered, "That fella, Dr. Spock . . ."

Someone asked, "what about Spock?"

"Well," Duke answered, "just let's forget him. He's down now. No use steppin' on him . . . The horrible part is, he isn't accepting it as punishment. He's wearin' it like a badge."

After a few more swigs of his screwdriver, Wayne went after the liberals.

"If there just weren't too many articulate left-wingers," he shook his head. "Trouble today is that most of the communications are in the hands of what semantics calls liberals. They are really radicals."

He said the situation had gotten that way through "permissiveness" and went on to say that "most of 'em in communications never finished college. I can see entering college as a Socialist, but if you leave college as a Socialist you're out of your head."

Another pause, another swallow of the screwdriver, and Wayne was talking about the kids of the nation.

"Y' know, when I was a kid we had pills, too. Ten of 'em cost a dollar. Fellas 'd take forty of these and go on a trip.

Only thing today is, you people make them important. You listen' to these punks. We had hippies in my day. Used to call 'em bindlestiffs. These bastards never took a bath and lived down by the tracks."

Martin got to saying how nobody writes about the good kids anymore. "How about the 4-H Clubs?" he asked. "How about the kinds that finish school, try out for the Olympics? I go past UCLA every day and I see kids out there running around the track."

Wayne ordered another screwdriver and promised Tony it would be "positively my last one." But he had one more thought he wanted to express.

"We were brought up on things like *Ivanhoe* and *Henry VIII*," he said. "The Crusades and things with guts to them. Now, instead, you hear "John and Mary Going Around San Pedro Harbor" 'stead of things with guts to them like we used to read."

He was asked about the ghettos.

"What about the ghettos?" he snapped. "I didn't think I'd live to look on television and see the most magnificent city in the U.S. and see cops standin' around while all that lootin' was goin' on without God-given law to use on 'em."

Tony Martin urged John Wayne to leave. The Duke's departure was halted by a waitress who wanted his autograph. Then Holmes Alexander, who does a newspaper column in the South, came over to shake Wayne's hand.

"You sure gave 'em a real good goin' over this morning," Alexander said. "Those liberal book-burners."

"Thank you," Big Duke smiled. Then with a wave of his hand, he left the bar.

Nobody had any doubts anymore about John Wayne's political stance, and it seemed certain that he was going to root Richard Nixon in as the next President—especially after witnessing the disgrace and bloodshed that descended on the Democratic National Convention in Chicago.

Yet a day would come in the not-too-distant future when three reporters for the *London Sunday Times* wrote a book entitled *An American Melodrama*. This book was a detailed analysis of the 1968 Presidential race, and its authors put an interesting tidbit into the eleventh chapter, quoting an office worker in the headquarters of the third-party candidate, George Wallace, the then former governor of Alabama. The worker was talking about persons who contributed to Wallace's campaign.

"Perhaps the most surprising name," the authors say, "is that of John Wayne, who gave such an impassioned address to the Republican convention. According to one of the women in the department that handled contributions in Montgomery, the Duke sent three weekly checks for $10,000 each—the last one inscribed on the back, 'Sock it to 'em, George!' "

When Wayne was asked about this allegation, he denied it. He explained what had happened.

"I was approached by the Wallace forces to serve in the campaign," Duke said. "They suggested that I might even be the Vice Presidential nominee on the Wallace ticket. But I refused. Wallace, I suppose, had some sound ideas. But I've been a Nixon man for years. I supported Dick Nixon heavily . . ."

At a later time, Wayne revealed that he had also been approached by the Republicans to run as their senatorial candidate in California. The other U.S. Senate seat from California was held by George Murphy. With Wayne occupying the second seat, and Reagan in the Governor's Mansion, the film capital would have a monopoly of the state's three highest elective offices.

But Wayne refused.

"I'm not a political animal," he apologized.

Nobody believed him, of course.

CHAPTER XXI

True Grit

It was now 1969.

John Wayne was in his fortieth year as an actor, his thirtieth year as a star, and his twentieth year in domination of the top-ten lists in grosses and popularity—and no one else could make that claim.

He was making $1 million a picture—plus 10 percent—and he was riding high. He had never won an Academy Award, but as he often put it:

"I'd like one but if I never win one, what the hell . . . I've made my mark no matter how you look at it."

In early 1969, John Wayne read another book. It was a still unpublished novel called *True Grit*. Wayne wanted to buy the book and offered up to $300,000, but producer Hal Wallis got to the author, Charles Portis, first. Duke not only wanted to play the role of the one-eyed U.S. Marshal, Rooster Cogburn, who, as he says, "was a mean old bastard that was me," but he also wanted to direct the film.

Now it was Wallis's property and the Duke had to make his deal with Hal cautiously.

"Okay," Wallis told Wayne, "you can play Cogburn but Hathaway's going to direct it."

"I'm convinced the part is like me," Wayne said. "Of course, it could be Lee Marvin, but he might make it too theatrical. I can get away with a little theatricality because I seldom use it."

There were no arguments from Wallis or Hathaway. Big Duke had the role of the drunken, gunslinging, one-eyed hero of *True Grit.*

When John Wayne went off to Colorado with his costars, Glen Campbell, Kim Darby, and Jeremy Slate, to film the picture, he played the role of the rascally, disreputable Rooster Cogburn, a fat old man, as if he himself had aged and fattened over the years to become the distillation of this federal marshal.

When the shooting was done, Wayne admitted that his role in the film had been his first chance since *Stagecoach* to play a character role into which he put his heart and soul.

Wayne was pleased beyond all expectations with the way Hathaway directed the film, the way he used backgrounds which "became almost a fantasy." Duke was particularly enthralled with the scene in which old Rooster faced four men across the meadow—and took the reins in his teeth and charged them.

"That's Henry at work," Wayne said. "It's a real meadow, but it looks almost dreamlike. Henry made it a fantasy and yet he kept it an honest Western."

In the end, when the film was finished, edited, distributed, and premiered—the true hero of *True Grit* was John Duke Wayne.

Several months later, he learned that the Academy of Motion Picture Arts and Sciences had selected him as one of the five nominees for an Oscar for the best performance by an actor in 1969.

John Wayne was rightly pleased—but his hopes didn't rise too high. He readily admitted that he expected a putdown from the not-so-silent liberal majority of movie performers. Wayne felt that outside of such celebrities as Walter Brennan, Yvonne DeCarlo, Robert Stack, Bob Cummings, and a handful of others, most performers in the movie capital repeatedly had displayed an unmistakable animus against his politics.

The difficulty of winning an Oscar because of the anti-crowd was not nearly as significant to Wayne as the fact that he was up against some of the toughest competition. Jon Voight and Dustin Hoffman had been nominated for their superb performances in *Midnight Cowboy*; Richard Burton was another candidate for his great role in *Anne of the Thousand Days*; and Peter O'Toole for his unforgettable enactment in *Goodbye, Mr. Chips*.

On the night of April 7, 1970, John Wayne attended the Academy Awards with Pilar in the Los Angeles Music Center. When it came time to announce the winner of the best actor award, Barbra Streisand had the task of ripping open the envelope and calling out John Wayne's name.

He went up on wobbly legs, received the award tremblingly, thanked everyone on a choked voice, and cracked, "Wow!"

His eyes were misty. He swallowed hard.

"If I'd a known that," he stammered, referring to his role as the whisky-soaked, one-eyed marshal, "I'd a put on a patch thirty-five years earlier."

Then he thanked everyone again and went off backstage.

"I didn't think I would get excited," he told well-wishers, "but when they called my name I didn't know whether to get up or run. You just can't help it. I'm damn pleased to have won it . . ."

Winnin' the Academy Award wasn't the livin' end for John Wayne. It was only another milestone in his career. Even before he won the coveted prize he'd filmed two more first-class films, *Undefeated* and *Chisum*, and then went off with Pilar and the children on an extended three-week vacation to the 26 Bar Ranch near Stanfield, Arizona, where pure-bred bulls are raised. In 1968 in Albuquerque, New Mexico, one of the bulls raised there, a yearling named 26 Mischief B98, was awarded the champion's blue ribbon at the Register of Merit Hereford Show at the State Fair.

The Arizona ranch, a spread of 17,000 irrigated acres with 40,000 head of cattle and 3,500 acres of cotton, is owned by John Wayne.

Chisum was based on the life of John Simpson Chisum, who in the 1870s was a famous cattle baron. John Wayne had now become, among many other things, a twentieth-century cattle baron.

Meanwhile, back in Washington, the President of the United States expressed admiration for a film he had just seen. Only once before had Richard Nixon commented about a movie, and that one was *Patton*. This time Mr. Nixon said he had viewed a picture in the White House theater which really grabbed him.

"I wondered why it is that the Westerns survive year after

year," said the President. "Perhaps one of the reasons, in addition to the excitement, the gun play, and the rest is that the good guys come out ahead in the Westerns, the bad guys lose."

Richard Nixon's four-star favorite was *Chisum*, and the nation's "First Reviewer" found that the film offered a healthy antidote to the sort of "glorification" of criminals and accused criminals which he believed the mass media had been guilty of in the coverage of such sensational trials as the Sharon Tate murder case.

Following *Chisum*, Wayne went into production of *Rio Lobo*, a nice family Western aimed at *True Grit* audiences, though not as good because Duke didn't have a Kim Darby. Then he played in *Big Jake*, flanked by his son Patrick, Chris Mitchum (Big Bob's boy), and Bruce Cabot as an Indian, as they close in on the kidnappers of Wayne's movie grandson, his eight-year-old real-life son John Ethan Wayne.

The shadowy stealth, a church tower, a killer Collie, a flashing machete, and the spitting guns added up to a horrifying drama—with another son, Michael, as the producer.

Toward the end of 1970, John Wayne finally consented to do his first television special for the National Broadcasting Company. It was a ninety-minute musical-comedy salute to our country entitled *Swing Out, Sweet Land*, featuring such stars as Glen Campbell singing "This is a Great Country"; Dan Blocker playing an Indian who sold Peter Minuit Manhattan Island for twenty-four dollars worth of trinkets (and returned two dollars to middle-man Wayne, cracking: "Thank you, tall man. Will see much of you in movies"); Bob Hope in a sketch of the Boston Tea Party ("I had breakfast with Benedict Arnold. He said, 'What'll you have'? and I said, 'Eggs Benedict.' ''); and many other stars in scenes of the Liberty Bell and other historic-patriotic landmarks.

It was a show that only a John Wayne could have emceed, a man a nation could instantly recognize not only as a superstar—but as a superpatriot. The map of the United States was his stage and no man seemed to have a better stance in that spot than the Big Duke.

A couple of weeks later, TV critic Kay Gardella made this observation in the *New York Daily News*:

"Not only was this salute to America the highest rated television special of the year, and the No. 1 in the last Nielsen report, it hit the jackpot on mail in this department. John Wayne, one of Hollywood's top box-office attractions, could conceivably walk off with the TV laurels for any season if he were around often enough . . .''

In early 1971, John Wayne went to Governor Reagan's second inaugural in Sacramento's Memorial Auditorium and served as master of ceremonies at the event, which featured such stars as Jack Benny, Buddy Ebsen, Dean Martin, James Stewart—and even a tranquil Frank Sinatra.

On leaving, it was John Wayne's turn to get hot under the collar. He ran into a group of Vietnam War protesters outside who were waving Vietcong flags. When the Big Duke spotted them, he was so outraged that he charged into them with fists flailing.

"You dirty no good bastards!" Wayne screamed at the protesters.

Gregory Kirkwood, twenty-two, one of *them*, filed a complaint with the police the next day seeking to have Wayne charged with disturbing the peace. Nothing came of Kirkwood's charge, and the case was quickly dropped after District Attorney John M. Price refused to prosecute Wayne.

"Mr. Wayne," said Price, "was exercising free speech when he shouted at the demonstrators."

It was a typical ending, in the tradition of a John Wayne movie. The Big Duke was the winner, as always.

CHAPTER XXII

The Last Cowboy?

This has been the story of a boy born Marion Michael Morrison who grew up to be John Wayne, the Big Duke—and more accurately the Iron Duke.

For more than forty years he has been climbing the mountain. He has scaled to the cinematic heavens and today he stands Everest tall above them all. He's the all-time box-office champ and no matter who came 'fore or after him—Clark Gable, Gary Cooper, Rudolph Valentino, Humphrey Bogart, Spencer Tracy, James Stewart, Douglas Fairbanks, Tom Mix—no one ever achieved the stature or success of this colossus of the silver screen.

He is Atlas and Cyclops and Polyphemus, Titan and Hercules, Goliath and Samson all wrapped up in one, and yet he is not a mythical being of more than human size and strength, but merely a very real person who lives among us today, who has influenced our world of entertainment as perhaps no man has, and who has swamped us with a tidal wave of candor about his politics and patriotism.

In nearly 150 films, he has reigned as the rugged frontiersman, the cowboy, the man sitting tall in the saddle, one of the screen's immortal cactus heroes, riding herd over the Western ranges of movie screens for more than four decades.

Only Gary Cooper before him had prevailed as the Supreme Man of the West; but there's no more Coop, and John Wayne still rides with the galloping posses, the reverberating hoofbeats, the blazing fire of guns, the roundups, and the fading sunsets.

His vigor is undiminished though the march of time has crinkled and cracked his face. His waist has ballooned and his gunbelt disappears into his gut, but he's still the fastest trigger in the West—and the best.

He survived two broken marriages, but the heartache and harangue that he experienced did not discourage or deter him from finding what looks like permanent connubial happiness in a third marriage. As family men go, no one has been a better father to his children than the Big Duke.

We said a while back that we'd give you a final report on Duke's grandchildren, but this, too, is subject to change from one minute to the next. As of now he has nineteen grandchildren—but the end is nowhere in sight.

Big Duke knows he's been lucky in life, and fortunate indeed to have beaten the Big C. He often speaks about that bout with cancer . . .

"I thought of three things when I had the operation—my

wife, my kids, and death. I was butchered. One lung gone, some of the other cut away. But I have huge lungs, so I'm almost back to capacity.

"When the doctor came in to give me the news, I sat in bed trying to be John Wayne and I gruffly said, 'Doctor, you tryin' to tell me I've got cancer?' What a shock. I didn't believe I was dying.

"People resist death. There's a little pull somewhere in you that begins wanting to stick around a little longer. I felt that pull every time I thought it was over. I was lucky. I beat it. The five years have passed and the doctors say I no longer have cancer. Now all I can feel is life."

Asked whether he plans to retire, he scoffs at the suggestion.

"Hell, I'm only goin' on sixty-five," drawls the biggest box-office attraction of all time. "Don't mention retirement to me."

Nobody does—since he won the Academy Award for *True Grit*. The way he feels now, he wants to go on and win another Oscar, and another . . .

His toupe may be getting larger, and it may take him longer to mount a horse, or to recover from a hangover, but so long as he can move around, John Wayne will be out there in front of the camera performing.

When Gary Cooper rode into the sunset, he left a legacy as a friend to the righteous, a hero to children, a flytrap to women—and a fortune for producers who had realized a $200 million gross on the ninety-five films he made in his forty years as an actor.

John Wayne is still gallopin' across the range, crawlin' on the beach at Iwo Jima, defendin' the Alamo, shootin' Indians, ropin' steers, battlin' ornery hombres, fightin' the

Vietcong, and wrestlin' the dragon of evil on land, sea, and in the air.

He is the George Herman Ruth of filmdom. Even the Babe's 714-homer record, which seemed unassailable for so many years, is now within the reach of Hank Aaron and Willie Mays. But who will ever top Duke Wayne's $400 million gross at the box office?

So long as John Wayne is up there on that wide, wide screen, or even on that constricted 295-square-inch bubble of glass, he will activate my sweat glands, force my adrenalin to flow, palpitate my heart, and even stir up my bowels.

There ain't none like 'im, I say. For, sad to add, the Iron Duke is the only real man of Hollywood who's left.

And yet, I know, it is just too much to hope—that John Wayne will never wane.

A John Wayne Filmography

1. **MOTHER MACHREE**
   (Fox)
   October, 1928. Directed by John Ford. With Belle Bennett, Neil Hamilton, Phillippe De Lacy. 75 min.

2. **FOUR SONS**
   (Fox)
   February, 1928. Directed by John Ford. With Margaret Mann, James Hall, Charles Morton. 100 min.

3. **HANGMAN'S HOUSE**
   (Fox)
   May, 1928. Directed by John Ford. With Victor McLaglen, Hobart Bosworth, June Collyer. 6,430 ft.

4. **SALUTE**
   (Fox)
   September, 1929. Directed by John Ford. With George O'Brien, Helen Chandler, Stepin Fetchit. 86 min.

5. **MEN WITHOUT WOMEN**
   (Fox)
   January, 1930. Directed by John Ford. With Kenneth MacKenna, Frank Albertson, Paul Page. 77 min.

6. **ROUGH ROMANCE**
   (Fox)
   May, 1930. Directed by A. F. Erickson. With George O'Brien, Helen Chandler, Antonio Moreno. 4,800 ft.

7. **THE BIG TRAIL**
   (Fox)
   November, 1930. Directed by Raoul Walsh. With Marguerite Churchill, David Rollins, El Brendel, Tully Marshall. 122 min.

8. **GIRLS DEMAND EXCITEMENT**
   (Fox)
   February, 1931. Directed by Seymour Felix. With Virginia Cherrill, Marguerite Churchill, Helen Jerome. 66 min.

9. **3 GIRLS LOST**
    (Fox)
    April, 1931. Directed by Sidney Lanfield. With Loretta Young, Lew Cody, Joyce Compton. 71 min.

10. **MEN ARE LIKE THAT**
    (Columbia)
    June, 1931. Directed by George B. Seitz. With Laura La Plante, June Clyde, Forrest Stanley. 67 min.

11. **RANGE FEUD**
    (Columbia)
    December, 1931. Directed by D. Ross Lederman. With Buck Jones, Susan Fleming, Ed LeSaint. 56 min.

12. **MAKER OF MEN**
    (Columbia)
    December, 1931. Directed by Edward Sedgwick. With Jack Holt, Joan Marsh, Richard Cromwell. 67 min.

13. **SHADOW OF THE EAGLE**
    (Mascot)
    February, 1932. Directed by Ford Beebe. With Dorothy Gulliver, Lloyd Whitlock, Edward Hearn, Pat O'Malley, Richard Tucker. 12 episodes.

14. **TEXAS CYCLONE**
    (Columbia)
    February, 1932. Directed by D. Ross Lederman. With Tim McCoy, Shirley Grey, Walter Brennan. 63 min.

15. **TWO-FISTED LAW**
    (Columbia)
    June, 1932. Directed by D. Ross Lederman. With Tim McCoy, Alice Day, Wheeler Oakman. 57 min.

16. **LADY AND GENT**
    (Paramount)
    July, 1932. Directed by Stephen Roberts. With George Bancroft, Wynne Gibson, Charles Starrett. 80 min.

17. **HURRICANE EXPRESS**
    (*Mascot*)
    August, 1932. Directed by Armand L. Schaefer and J. P. McGowan. With Shirley Grey, J. Farrell MacDonald, Tully Marshall, Conway Tearle. 12 chapters.

18. **RIDE HIM COWBOY**
    (*Warner Brothers*)
    August, 1932. Directed by Fred Allen. With Ruth Hall, Henry B. Walthall. 56 min.

19. **THE BIG STAMPEDE**
    (*Warner Brothers*)
    October, 1932. Directed by Tenny Wright. With Noah Beery, Sr., Mae Madison. 54 min.

20. **HAUNTED GOLD**
    (*Warner Brothers*)
    December, 1932. Directed by Mack V. Wright. With Sheila Terry, Erville Alderson, Harry Woods. 58 min.

21. **THE TELEGRAPH TRAIL**
    (*Warner Brothers*)
    March, 1933. Directed by Tenny Wright. With Marceline Day, Frank McHugh, Otis Harlan. 55 min.

22. **THE THREE MUSKETEERS**
    (*Mascot*)
    April, 1933. Directed by Armand L. Schaefer and Colbert Clark. With Ruth Hall, Raymond Hatton, Noah Berry, Jr., Jack Mulhall. 12 chapters.

23. **CENTRAL AIRPORT**
    (*First National*)
    April, 1933. Directed by William Wellman. With Richard Barthelmess, Sally Eilers, Tom Brown. 75 min.

24. **SOMEWHERE IN SONORA**
    (*Warner Brothers*)
    May, 1933. Directed by Mack V. Wright. With Shirley Palmer, H. B. Walthall, J. P. McGowan. 57 min.

25. **THE LIFE OF JIMMY DOLAN**
    (Warner Brothers)
    June, 1933. Directed by Archie Mayo. With Douglas Fairbanks, Jr., Loretta Young, Aline MacMahon. 70 min.

26. **HIS PRIVATE SECRETARY**
    (Showmans Pictures)
    June, 1933. Directed by Phil H. Whitman. With Evalyn Knapp, Alec B. Francis, Reginald Barlow. 60 min.

27. **BABY FACE**
    (Warners Brothers)
    July, 1933. Directed by Alfred E. Green. With Barbara Stanwyck, George Brent, Donald Cook. 74 min.

28. **THE MAN FROM MONTEREY**
    (Warner Brothers)
    July, 1933. Directed by Mack V. Wright. With Ruth Hall, Luis Alberni, Francis Ford. 57 min.

29. **RIDERS OF DESTINY**
    (Monogram)
    October, 1933. Directed by Robert N. Bradbury. With Cecilia Parker, George Hayes, Forrest Taylor. 58 min.

30. **COLLEGE COACH**
    (Warner Brothers)
    November, 1933. Directed by William Wellman. With Dick Powell, Pat O'Brien, Ann Dvorak. 75 min.

31. **SAGEBRUSH TRAIL**
    (Monogram)
    December, 1933. Directed by Armand Schaefer. With Nancy Shubert, Lane Chandler, Yakima Canutt. 55 min.

32. **THE LUCKY TEXAN**
    (Monogram)
    January, 1934. Directed by Robert N. Bradbury. With Barbara Sheldon, George Hayes, Lloyd Whitlock. 56 min.

33. **WEST OF THE DIVIDE**
    (Monogram)
    March, 1934. Directed by Robert N. Bradbury. With Virginia Brown Faire, Lloyd Whitlock, George Hayes. 55 min.

34. **BLUE STEEL**
(Monogram)
May, 1934. Directed by Robert N. Bradbury. With Eleanor Hunt, George Hayes, Ed Peil. 54 min.

35. **THE MAN FROM UTAH**
(Monogram)
May, 1934. Directed by Robert N. Bradbury. With Polly Ann Young, George Hayes, Yakima Canutt. 55 min.

36. **RANDY RIDES ALONE**
(Monogram)
June, 1934. Directed by Harry Fraser. With Alberta Vaughn, George Hayes, Yakima Canutt. 53 min.

37. **THE STAR PACKER**
(Monogram)
July, 1934. Directed by Robert N. Bradbury. With Verna Hillie, George Hayes, Yakima Canutt. 54 min.

38. **THE TRAIL BEYOND**
(Monogram)
October, 1934. Directed by Robert N. Bradbury. With Verna Hillie, Noah Beery, Sr., Noah Beery, Jr., Iris Lancaster. 55 min.

39. **THE LAWLESS FRONTIER**
(Monogram)
November, 1934. Directed by Robert N. Bradbury. With Sheila Terry, George Hayes, Earl Dwire. 54 min.

40. **'NEATH ARIZONA SKIES**
(Monogram)
December, 1934. Directed by Harry Frazer. With Sheila Terry, Jay Wilsey, Shirley Rickets. 52 min.

41. **TEXAS TERROR**
(Monogram)
February, 1935. Directed by Robert N. Bradbury. With Lucille Brown, LeRoy Mason, George Hayes. 45 min.

42. **RAINBOW VALLEY**
    (Monogram)
    March, 1935. Directed by Robert N. Bradbury. With Lucille
    Brown, LeRoy Mason, George Hayes. 52 min.

43. **THE DESERT TRAIL**
    (Monogram)
    April, 1935. Directed by Lewis Collins. With Mary Korman, Paul
    Fix, Edward Chandler. 58 min.

44. **THE DAWN RIDER**
    (Monogram)
    June, 1935. Directed by Robert N. Bradbury. With Marion
    Burns, Yakima Canutt, Reed Howes. 56 min.

45. **PARADISE CANYON**
    (Monogram)
    July, 1935. Directed by Carl Pierson. With Marion Burns, Earle
    Hodgins, Yakima Canutt. 52 min.

46. **WESTWARD HO!**
    (Republic)
    August, 1935. Directed by Robert N. Bradbury. With Sheila
    Manners, Frank McGlynn, Jr., Jack Curtis. 60 min.

47. **THE NEW FRONTIER**
    (Republic)
    October, 1935. Directed by Carl Pierson. With Muriel Evans,
    Murdock MacQuarries, Alan Cavan. 59 min.

48. **THE OREGON TRAIL**
    (Republic)
    January, 1936. Directed by Scott Pembroke. With Ann Ruther-
    ford, Joe Girand, Yakima Canutt. 59 min.

49. **LAWLESS RANGE**
    (Republic)
    February, 1936. Directed by Robert N. Bradbury. With Sheila
    Manners, Frank McGlynn, Jr., Earl Dwire. 54 min.

50. **THE LAWLESS NINETIES**
    (Republic)
    February, 1936. Directed by Joseph Kane. With Ann Ruther-
    ford, Harry Woods, George Hayes. 55 min.

51. **KING OF THE PECOS**
    (Republic)
    March, 1936. Directed by Joseph Kane. With Muriel Evans, Cy Kendall, Jack Clifford. 6 reels.

52. **THE LONELY TRAIL**
    (Republic)
    May, 1936. Directed by Joseph Kane. With Ann Rutherford, Cy Kendall, Bob Kortman. 58 min.

53. **WINDS OF THE WASTELAND**
    (Republic)
    July, 1936. Directed by Mack V. Wright. With Phyllis Fraser, Yakima Canutt, Douglas Cosgrove. 57 min.

54. **THE SEA SPOILERS**
    (Universal)
    September, 1936. Directed by Frank Strayer. With Nan Grey, Fuzzy Knight, William Bakewell. 63 min.

55. **CONFLICT**
    (Universal)
    November, 1936. Directed by David Howard. With Jean Rogers, Tommy Bupp, Eddie Borden. 60 min.

56. **CALIFORNIA STRAIGHT AHEAD**
    (Universal)
    May, 1937. Directed by Arthur Lubin. With Louise Latimer, Robert McWade, Tully Marshall. 67 min.

57. **I COVER THE WAR**
    (Universal)
    July, 1937. Directed by Arthur Lubin. With Gwen Gaze, Don Barclay, Pat Somerset. 68 min.

58. **IDOL OF THE CROWDS**
    (Universal)
    October, 1937. Directed by Arthur Lubin. With Shelia Bromley, Charles Brokaw, Billy Burrud. 65 min.

59. **ADVENTURE'S END**
    (*Universal*)
    December, 1937. Directed by Arthur Lubin. With Diana Gibson, Moroni Olsen, Montague Love. 63 min.

60. **BORN TO THE WEST**
    (*Paramount*)
    December, 1937. Directed by Charles Barton. With Marsha Hunt, James Craig, Johnny Mack Brown. 66 min.

61. **PALS OF THE SADDLE**
    (*Republic*)
    August, 1938. Directed by George Sherman. With Ray Corrigan, Max Terhune, Doreen McKay. 55 min.

62. **OVERLAND STAGE RAIDERS**
    (*Republic*)
    September, 1938. Directed by George Sherman. With Ray Corrigan, Max Terhune, Louis Brooks. 55 min.

63. **SANTA FE STAMPEDE**
    (*Republic*)
    November, 1938. Directed by George Sherman. With Ray Corrigan, Max Terhune, June Martel. 56 min.

64. **RED RIVER RANGE**
    (*Republic*)
    December 1938. Directed by George Sherman. With Ray Corrigan, Max Terhune, Lorna Gray. 56 min.

65. **STAGECOACH**
    (*United Artists*)
    March, 1939. Directed by John Ford. With Claire Trevor, Tim Holt, George Bancroft, Andy Devine, Thomas Mitchell, John Carratine, Donald Meek, 97 min.

66. **THE NIGHT RIDERS**
    (*Republic*)
    April, 1939. Directed by George Sherman. With Ray Corrigan, Max Terhune, Dorreen McKay. 58 min.

67. **THREE TEXAS STEERS**
    (*Republic*)
    May, 1939. Directed by George Sherman. With Ray Corrigan,
    Max Terhune, Carole Landis. 57 min.

68. **WYOMING OUTLAW**
    (*Republic*)
    June, 1939. Directed by George Sherman. With Ray Corrigan,
    Raymond Hatton, Adele Pearce. 56 min.

69. **NEW FRONTIER**
    (*Republic*)
    August, 1939. Directed by George Sherman. With Ray Corrigan, Raymond Hatton, Phyllis Isley. 57 min.

70. **ALLEGHENY UPRISING**
    (*RKO*)
    November, 1939. Directed by William A. Seiter. With Claire
    Trevor, Brain Donlevy, George Sanders. 81 min.

71. **THE DARK COMMAND.**
    (*Republic*)
    April, 1940. Directed by Raoul Walsh. With Claire Trevor, Walter Pidgeon, George Hayes. 94 min.

72. **THREE FACES WEST**
    (*Republic*)
    July, 1940. Directed by Bernard Vorhaus. With Sigrid Gurie,
    Charles Coburn, Spencer Charters. 81 min.

73. **SEVEN SINNERS**
    (*Universal*)
    October, 1940. Directed by Tay Garnett. With Marlene Dietrich, Broderick Crawford, Mischa Auer. 86 min.

74. **MELODY RANCH**
    (*Republic*)
    November, 1940. Directed by Joseph Stantley. With Gene
    Autry, Jimmy Durante, Ann Miller. 84 min.

75. **THE LONG VOYAGE HOME**
    (*United Artists*)
    November, 1940. Directed by John Ford. With Thomas Mitchell, Ian Hunter, Wilfred Lawson, Barry Fitzgerald, Ward Bond, 105 min.

76. **A MAN BETRAYED**
    (*Republic*)
    March, 1941. Directed by John H. Auer. With Frances Dee, Edward Ellis, Wallace Ford. 80 min.

77. **THE LADY FROM LOUISIANA**
    (*Republic*)
    April, 1941. Directed by Bernard Vorhaus. With Ona Munson, Ray Middleton, Henry Stephenson. 82 min.

78. **THE SHEPHERD OF THE HILLS**
    (*Paramount*)
    July, 1941. Directed by Henry Hathaway. With Betty Field, Harry Carey, Sr., Beulah Bondi. 95 min.

79. **LADY FOR A NIGHT**
    (*Republic*)
    January, 1942. Directed by Leigh Jason. With Joan Blondell, Ray Middleton, Phillip Merivale. 88 min.

80. **REAP THE WILD WIND**
    (*Paramount*)
    March, 1942. Directed by Cecil B. DeMille. With Paulette Goddard, Ray Milland, Susan Hayward. 124 min.

81. **THE SPOILERS**
    (*Universal*)
    May, 1942. Directed by Frank Lloyd. With Marlene Dietrich, Randolph Scott, Margaret Lindsay. 85 min.

82. **IN OLD CALIFORNIA**
    (*Republic*)
    May, 1942. Directed by William McGann. With Binnie Barnes, Albert Dekker, Helen Parrish. 88 min.

83. **THE FLYING TIGERS**
    (*Republic*)
    October, 1942. Directed by David Miller. With Anna Lee, John Carroll, Paul Kelly. 102 min.

84. **REUNION IN FRANCE**
    (MGM)
    December, 1942. Directed by Jules Dassin. With Joan Crawford, Phillip Dorn, Ann Ayars. 102 min.

85. **PITTSBURGH**
    (Universal)
    December, 1942. Directed by Lewis Seiler. With Marlene Dietrich, Randolph Scott, Frank Craven. 93 min.

86. **A LADY TAKES A CHANCE**
    (RKO)
    September, 1943. Directed by William A. Seiter. With Jean Arthur, Charles Winninger, Phil Silvers. 86 min.

87. **IN OLD OKLAHOMA**
    (Republic)
    December, 1943. Directed by Albert S. Rogell. With Martha Scott, Albert Dekker, George Hayes. 102 min.

88. **THE FIGHTING SEABEES**
    (Republic)
    March, 1944. Directed by Edward Ludwig and Howard Lydecker. With Susan Hayward, Dennis O'Keefe, William Frawley. 100 min.

89. **TALL IN THE SADDLE.**
    (RKO)
    October, 1944. Directed by Edward L. Marin. With Ella Raines, Ward Bond, George Hayes. 87 min.

90. **THE FLAME OF THE BARBARY COAST**
    (Republic)
    April, 1945. Directed by Joseph Kane. With Ann Dvorak, Joseph Schildkraut, William Frawley. 91 min.

91. **BACK TO BATAAN**
    (RKO)
    May, 1945. Directed by Edward Dmytrk. With Anthony Quinn, Beulah Bondi, Fely Franquelli. 97 min.

92. **THEY WERE EXPENDABLE**
    (MGM)
    December, 1945. Directed by John Ford. With Robert Montgomery, Donna Reed, Ward Bond, Jack Holt, Leon Ames. 136 min.

93. **DAKOTA**
    (Republic)
    December, 1945. Directed by Joseph Kane. With Vera Ralston, Walter Brennan, Ward Bond. 82 min.

94. **WITHOUT RESERVATIONS**
    (RKO)
    May, 1946. Directed by Mervyn Le Roy. With Claudette Colbert, Don Defore, Anne Triola. 107 min.

95. **ANGEL AND THE BADMEN**
    (Republic)
    February, 1947. Directed by James Edward Grant. With Gail Russell, Harry Carey, Sr., Bruce Cabot. 100 min.

96. **TYCOON**
    (RKO)
    December, 1947. Directed by Richard Wallace. With Laraine Day, Sir Cedric Hardwicke, Judith Anderson. 126 min.

97. **FORT APACHE**
    (RKO)
    March, 1948. Directed by John Ford. With Henry Fonda, Shirley Temple, John Agar. 127 min.

98. **RED RIVER**
    (United Artists)
    September, 1948. Directed by Howard Hawks. With Montgomery Clift, Joanne Dru, Walter Brennan. 125 min.

99. **3 GODFATHERS**
    (MGM)
    January, 1949. Directed by John Ford. With Ward Bond, Pedro Armendariz, Mae Marsh. 106 min.

100. **WAKE OF THE RED WITCH**
     (Republic)
     March, 1949. Directed by Edward Ludwig. With Gail Russell,
     Gig Young, Adele Mara. 106 min.

101. **THE FIGHTING KENTUCKIAN**
     (Republic)
     October, 1949. Directed by George Waggner. With Vera Ral-
     ston, Philip Dorn, Oliver Hardy. 100 min.

102. **SHE WORE A YELLOW RIBBON**
     (RKO)
     October, 1949. Directed by John Ford. With Joanne Dru, John
     Agar, Ben Johnson. 103 min.

103. **SANDS OF IWO JIMA**
     (Republic)
     March, 1950. Directed by Allan Dwan. With Adele Mara, John
     Agar, Forrest Tucker. 109 min.

104. **JET PILOT**
     (RKO U-I)
     September, 1957. Directed by Joseph Von Sternberg. With Ja-
     net Leigh, Hans Conreid, Richard Rober. 113 min.

105. **RIO GRANDE**
     (Republic)
     November, 1950. Directed by John Ford. With Maureen
     O'Hara, Ben Johnston, Claude Jarman, Jr. 105 min.

106. **OPERATION PACIFIC**
     (Warner Brothers)
     January, 1951. Directed by George Waggner. With Patricia
     Neal, Ward Bond, Scott Forbes. 110 min.

107. **THE BULLFIGHTER AND THE LADY**
     (Republic)
     May, 1951. Directed by Budd Boetticher. With Robert Stack,
     Gilbert Roland. 87 min.

108. **FLYING LEATHERNECKS**
     (RKO)
     August, 1951. Directed by Nicholas Ray. With Robert Ryan,
     Don Taylor, Janis Carter. 102 min.

109. **BIG JIM McLAIN**
(Warner Brothers)
August, 1952. Directed by Edward Ludwig. With James Arness, Nancy Olson, Alan Napier. 90 min.

110. **THE QUIET MAN**
(Republic)
December, 1952. Directed by John Ford. With Maureen O'Hara, Barry Fitzgerald, Victor McLaglen, Ward Bond, Mildred Natwick. 129 min.

111. **TROUBLE ALONG THE WAY**
(Warner Brothers)
April, 1953. Directed by Michael Curtiz. With Donna Reed, Charles Coburn, Tom Tully. 110 min.

112. **ISLAND IN THE SKY**
(Warner Brothers)
September, 1953. Directed by William A. Wellman. With Lloyd Nolan, Walter Abel, James Arness. 109 min.

113. **HONDO**
(Warner Brothers)
January, 1954. Directed by John Farrow and John Ford. With Geraldine Page, Ward Bond, Michael Pate. 83 min.

114. **THE HIGH AND THE MIGHTY**
(Warner Brothers)
July, 1954. Directed by William A. Wellman. With Loraine Day, Claire Trevor, Robert Stack. 147 min.

115. **THE SEA CHASE**
(Warner Brothers)
June, 1955. Directed by John Farrow. With Lana Turner, David Farrar, Lyle Bettger. 117 min.

116. **BLOOD ALLEY**
(Warner Brothers)
October, 1955. Directed by William A. Wellman. With Lauren Bacall, Anita Ekberg, Paul Fix. 115 min.

117. **THE CONQUEROR**
(RKO)
March, 1956. Directed by Dick Powell. With Susan Hayward, Pedro Armendariz, Agnes Moorehead. 111 min.

118. **THE SEARCHERS**
(Warner Brothers)
May, 1956. Directed by John Ford. With Vera Miles, Natalie Wood, Jeffrey Hunter. 119 min.

119. **WINGS OF THE EAGLES**
(MGM)
February, 1957. Directed by John Ford. With Maureen O'Hara, Dan Dailey, Ward Bond. 110 min.

120. **LEGEND OF THE LOST**
(United Artists)
December, 1957. Directed by Henry Hathaway. With Sophia Loren, Rossano Brazzi, Kurt Kasznar. 109 min.

121. **CHINA DOLL**
(United Artists)
August, 1958. Directed by Frank Borzac. With Victor Mature, Lili Has, Bob Mathias. 85 min.

122. **THE BARBARIAN AND GEISHA**
(Fox)
October, 1958. Directed by John Huston. With Sam Jaffe, Eiko Ando, So Yamamura. 104 min.

123. **RIO BRAVO**
(Warner Brothers)
April, 1959. Directed by Howard Hawks. With Angie Dickinson, Dean Martin, Walter Brennan, Ricky Nelson. 141 min.

124. **THE HORSE SOLDIERS**
(United Artists)
July, 1959. Directed by John Ford. With William Holden, Constance Towers, Althea Gibson.

125. **THE ALAMO**
(United Artists)
October, 1960. Directed by John Wayne and John Ford. With Linda Cristal, Richard Widmark, Laurence Harvey. 162 min.

126. **NORTH TO ALASKA**
(Fox)
November, 1960. Directed by Henry Hathaway. With Stewart Granger, Capucine, Ernie Kovacs. 122 min.

127. **THE COMANCHEROS**
(Fox)
November, 1961. Directed by Michael Curtiz. With Ina Balin, Stuart Whitman, Nehemiah Persoff. 107 min.

128. **THE MAN WHO SHOT LIBERTY VALANCE**
(Paramount)
April, 1962. Directed by John Ford. With James Stewart, Vera Miles, Lee Marvin. 122 min.

129. **HATARI**
(Paramount)
August, 1962. Directed by Howard Hawks. With Elsa Martinelli, Hardy Kruger, Michele Girardon. 159 min.

130. **HOW THE WEST WAS WON**
(MGM)
June, 1964. Directed by Henry Hathaway, John Ford, and George Marshall. With Carroll Baker, Carolyn Jones, George Peppard. 162 min.

131. **THE LONGEST DAY.**
(Fox)
June, 1963. Directed by Ken Annakin, Andrew Marton, and Bernhard Wicki. With Robert Mitchum, Henry Fonda, Robert Wagner. 180 min.

132. **DONOVAN'S REEF**
(Paramount)
July, 1963. Directed by John Ford. With Elizabeth Allen, Lee Marvin, Cesar Romero. 112 min.

133. **McLINTOCK**
(United Artists)
November, 1963. Directed by Andrew V. McLaglen. With Maureen O'Hara, Yvonne De Carlo, Patrick Wayne. 127 min.

134. **CIRCUS WORLD**
     (*Cinerama-Paramount*)
     April, 1965. Directed by Henry Hathaway. With Rita Hayworth, Claudia Cardinale, Lloyd Nolan. 138 min.

135. **THE GREATEST STORY EVER TOLD**
     (*United Artists*)
     February, 1965. Directed by George Stevens. With Max von Sydow, Charlton Heston, Jose Ferrer.

136. **IN HARMS WAY**
     (*Paramount*)
     June, 1965. Directed by Otto Preminger. With Jill Hayworth, Henry Fonda, Kirk Douglas. 165 min.

137. **THE SONS OF KATIE ELDER**
     (*Paramount*)
     July, 1965. Directed by Henry Hathaway. With Dean Martin, Martha Hyer, Earl Holliman. 122 min.

138. **CAST A GIANT SHADOW**
     (*United Artists*)
     April, 1966. Directed by Mel Shavelson. With Kirk Douglas, Yul Brynner, Senta Berger. 141 min.

139. **THE WAR WAGON**
     (*Universal*)
     June, 1967. Directed by Burt Kennedy. With Kirk Douglas, Howard Keel, Robert Walker. 101 min.

140. **EL DORADO**
     (*Paramount*)
     July, 1967. Directed by Howard Hawks. With Robert Mitchum, James Caan, Charlene Holt. 126. min.

141. **THE GREEN BERETS**
     (*Warner/7 Arts*)
     July, 1968. Directed by John Wayne, Ray Kellog, and Mervyn Le Roy. With David Janssen, Jim Hutton, Aldo Ray. 141 min.

142. **HELLFIGHTERS**
     (*Universal*)
     December, 1968. Directed by Andrew V. McLaglen. With Katherine Ross, Jim Hutton, Vera Miles. 121 min.

143. **TRUE GRIT**
     (*Paramount*)
     July, 1969. Directed by Henry Hathaway. With Kim Darby, Glen Campbell, Jeremy Slate. 128 min.

144. **UNDEFEATED**
     (*Fox*)
     November, 1969. Directed by Andrew V. McLaglen. With Rock Hudson, Lee Meriweather, Royal Dano, Bruce Cabot, Ben Johnson. 119 min.

145. **CHISUM**
     (*Warner/7 Arts*)
     1970. Directed by Andrew V. McLaglen. With Bruce Cabot, Richard Jaeckel, Forrest Tucker, Chris George. 111 min.

146. **RIO LOBO**
     (*National General*)
     1971. Directed by Howard Hawks. With George Rivero, Jack Elam, Jennifer O'Neil, George Plimpton. 114 min.

147. **THE COWBOYS**
     (*Warner Bros.*)
     1972. Directed by Mark Rydell. With Roscoe Lee Browne, Coleen Denhurst, Bruce Dern. 128 min.

Index